Revealing the Butterfly

Choosing godly transformation

Revealing the Butterfly

Choosing godly transformation

Sharon Prins

The Christadelphian
404 Shaftmoor Lane, Hall Green, Birmingham B28 8SZ, UK

2023

First published 2023

© 2023 The Christadelphian Magazine and Publishing Association

ISBN 978 0 85189 467 6 (print edition)
ISBN 978 0 85189 468 3 (electronic edition)

Cover: *Abi Sawell*

Printed and bound in the UK by
CMP (UK) Limited

Contents

Thanks!

THERE are a few people to whom I am extremely indebted for their help with this book. My awkward sentences, outdated words, poor use of punctuation, and general mistakes, have all needed correcting.

My thanks go to my wonderful husband who, besides my amazing God, has been my greatest cheerleader and encourager. He has given me that gentle push each time I've lost momentum, or have been tempted to give up. He has patiently helped me edit, proofread, restructure sentences, rewrite confusing concepts and learn the basics of using a computer for writing! I am so thankful for his help. I wouldn't have been able to do it without you, Robert!

I am so grateful to the two mums in my life. Their encouragement and support in all aspects of my life have been amazing. I really appreciate the time you have both taken to proofread and give helpful feedback.

Thank you to my two daughters: my elder daughter, who has read, supported, encouraged and given helpful feedback; my younger daughter who has patiently put up with me reading and re-reading this book to her through its various rewrites. I love you both dearly. Shine as your own amazing selves, and grow those butterfly wings of beautiful transformation!

I am thankful to Gail, who has given some very useful feedback, and taken the time to proofread, and help the book make sense. Your feedback during the early awkward formative stages of the book was invaluable.

Thank you Jess, for some much needed encouragement; a helpful prompt to keep pressing on. I appreciate your input. Thank you also for picking up the challenge to proofread and edit. You have done an amazing job of curbing my overly enthusiastic use of commas as well as giving some very helpful rewording suggestions. I appreciate your time and effort very much.

Thank you also to Ruth and Jackie for reading the draft copy and providing feedback. I appreciate it!

I am thankful to the editing team at Wilderness Voice, who have helped me see my script through new eyes, so that a more cohesive book could be formed. Thank you!

And lastly, I am truly most grateful to my wonderful God. He has prompted, enabled, and walked alongside me with this project. He has opened my eyes to His great love. He has nudged me in the right direction for needful change. He has given me Jesus to motivate, inspire and to walk close beside me.

"To him who is able to keep you from falling and to present you before his glorious presence without fault and with great joy – to the only God our Saviour be glory, majesty, power and authority, through Jesus Christ our Lord, before all ages, now and for evermore!" (Jude verses 24,25).

Introduction

I REALLY need some change in my life. I want to be more like the Lord Jesus.

At least, that was my intention and the general direction that I wanted my life to take when I first committed it to the Lord some years ago.

But it's been a bit of a struggle. I'm in a constant battle between a God-based life, and a Me-based life.

Way too often the Me-based life has the upper hand!

The Me-based life is my default setting. It is a built-in radar that is subconsciously looking for ways to gratify self, promote self, protect self, pursue self-interest and to consider my own needs above those of others. The Me-based life desires many of the things that the world has to offer, and it constantly wants more, and to be more.

The God-based life says I should let go of self, tear myself away from the world's hold, desire God's way, and be more like our Lord Jesus.

It's a hard choice to make, and an even harder thing to do!

It's not an altogether dismal outlook however. There is great reward and amazing fulfilment in choosing the God-based life. I do believe that. I just need some help to transition out of the Me-based setting!

That is why I need transformation. Transformation is a big word with big expectations. When something transforms, it goes through a process that creates a marked change in it, whether it be in form, nature or appearance.

Spiritual transformation for me, or you, will not bring about any physical change for us. It's a change to our character. It's an internal thing, rather than an external thing.

So this is a book written by a woman who needed to hear these things and be changed by them. It is a book written for women; with sympathy towards some of the struggles that women can encounter in their own pursuit of transformation. As a woman, we can often have complicated emotional insecurities going on. We have our places of vulnerability. We are thirsty for approval, love and acceptance. We want a sense of purpose. The desire to have these needs met often dictates how we live our lives, and how responsive we can be towards letting go of the Me-based life, and embracing the God-based life.

With all this in mind, please join me now on a journey of change. This change journey involves understanding our value. Our perspective of our self-worth impacts what our life journey looks like. We ultimately want a foundation that helps us realise that, although we are flawed, we are valuable. Although we are far from perfect, we are wanted and loved. As we learn to see the value and purpose that has been poured into us, we will find ourselves more open to releasing the unhealthy things that we have been holding tight to. We want a foundation that can help us open our hands to let go of 'Me'. We want a foundation that helps us keep our hands and heart open to receive Him.

Being more like our Lord Jesus is our ultimate goal in transformation.

I should mention that we will have some company along the way. We will be accompanied by some caterpillar friends. They are on a transformation journey too. Their journey is a very visual and external one, with changes to their form and feature. We will be able to track their change progress throughout the pages of this book.

They are on their way towards becoming a butterfly. In type, so are we.

Let's begin our change journey together.

Section One

Chapter 1

A tale of two butterflies

"Do not conform to the pattern of this world, but be transformed by the renewing of your mind. Then you will be able to test and approve what God's will is – his good, pleasing and perfect will" (Romans 12:2).

"Since, then, you have been raised with Christ, set your hearts on things above, where Christ is, seated at the right hand of God. Set your minds on things above, not on earthly things. For you died, and your life is now hidden with Christ in God. When Christ, who is your life, appears, then you also will appear with him in glory" (Colossians 3:1-4).

I WAS watching a butterfly that had just emerged from its chrysalis.

The butterfly sat on its leaf in the sunshine, drying its wings. The wings were crumpled and bent. The butterfly opened and closed its wings in an attempt to dry them off and have them expand. But the movement that was designed to pump life into the wings of a newly hatched butterfly was not having the desired effect for this little one. These were wings that would never fully expand. They would never enable their owner to take to the air. They were deformed. Something had gone wrong in the change process for this little creature. It was newly hatched, but incapable of being all it was designed to be.

I felt sorry for this butterfly that would never be able to fly.

There is something very sad about seeing new life emerge, only to find that it is unable to be all that it could be.

On another leaf, on another day, another Monarch butterfly began its transformed life. This butterfly had also emerged from its chrysalis; but with quite a different outcome. By the time I saw this butterfly, it was already well on the way towards having dry and expanded wings. The wings were uniform, vibrant and beautiful. They were strong, healthy wings which would soon be ready to take its owner on a journey to new heights and different places. Adventure and life were calling. It was ready to live out its life purpose, and be all that it was designed to be. The change process had gone as it should for this butterfly. It had a life full of potential in front of it. Soon it would fly away to do whatever butterflies do. Then, in due course, it would find its way to a nearby swan plant (milkweed) to lay the seed of new life. The eggs it would deposit on the plant would contain the potential to create more butterflies.

How satisfying it felt to watch this small creature begin its life of purpose. It was really beautiful. It felt so right.

God created butterflies with the amazing ability to change from one thing to another. From a tiny egg, to a caterpillar, to a chrysalis, to a butterfly; all these stages are a process of constant change. Metamorphosis. They are massive changes in the life of one small creature. How amazing it is that a small crawly thing like a caterpillar could turn into such a beautiful creature with wings!

When I think about transformation, I immediately think of butterflies. They are a beautiful illustration of visual transformation. That is why I have chosen butterflies as a picture of transformation for us. There are many aspects about the journey of change that a butterfly goes through that can have similarity to our own transformation journey. We will see this throughout the book.

We are always in a process of change. Physically we are different from when we were born. Our bodies have grown and changed. We are taller, wider, and in varying stages of physical maturity.

We have been changing mentally, emotionally and spiritually. Our life experiences, upbringings, world views and perspectives have all been influencing change to our mental, emotional and spiritual state.

Character is being formed based on how we have responded to our experiences in each area of our life.

Until the day we die, or our Lord Jesus returns, we are always going to be experiencing some sort of change. Change is a natural process, it's what life is all about. We are very different now from what we were when we were first born. In fact, we are so used to 'growing up' being such a natural part of life, that we would be very saddened were we to come across a person who remained a baby all their life!

Physical change doesn't leave us with much choice. We are mortal, which means the change process for us is one of decay. Our journey of spiritual change has more choice involved with it. Whatever we choose on this journey will change us, one way or another. Our choices have the ability to move us towards full and abundant life, or away from it. Our choices bring us either closer to God's heart, or further away from Him.

Here is what the Bible has to say about the biggest choice we will ever make in our lives:

"Do not conform any longer to the pattern of this world, but be transformed by the renewing of your mind. Then you will be able to test and approve what God's will is – his good, pleasing and perfect will" (Romans 12:2).

This verse tells us that we default to being conformed to the world. God is urging us to get out of this pattern and to choose instead the way of transformation, which begins with the renewing of our mind.

The Bible also tells us that staying conformed to the pattern of this world will lead to death and unfulfilled potential:

"Do not love the world or anything in the world. If anyone loves the world, the love of the Father is not in them. For everything in the world – the lust of the flesh, the lust of the eyes and the pride of life – comes not from the Father but from the world. The world and its desires pass away, but whoever does the will of God lives forever" (1 John 2:15-17).

Being conformed to the pattern of this world does not allow us to be anything like what God wants us to be. Rather, God wants us to choose the pathway of transformation, by being renewed in our mind. This choice will give us a new way of thinking, perceiving and acting.

So we have two butterflies. In our opening story, one butterfly had gone through its process of change, but could not become all it was meant to become. It could not fly because its wings were deformed. The other had achieved full and successful change to become a creature that could live its life as all that it was designed to be.

Sadly, butterflies have no choice as to how they will ultimately turn out.

But, thanks be to God, we do. We have a lot more choice about what we will ultimately look like.

Our ultimate goal will be to look like our Lord Jesus – in character, purpose and intention. This is the transformation result that

God wants for us. But this can only happen if we choose not to be conformed any longer to the world.

To choose not to be conformed to the world means we need to be willing to let go of 'self' – the selfish, self-centred, self-absorbed, self-gratifying, self-promoting parts of ourselves. This is our 'Me-based' setting.

This is easier said than done! As I have discovered, it is very difficult to rouse any motivation to let go of 'self', when I am battling with insecurities that cause me to put up a wall of self-protection. I put up walls to guard my heart from any pain that might be associated with anything that undermines my sense of worth. This causes me to have a clouded perception of what I should be willing to let go of, with regard to 'self', and what I should accept and nurture.

To be able to embrace transformation, I have need of both some healthy assurance of love and value, and the ability to discern what is unhealthy about myself.

This is going to require some help!

Some of the insecurities I have struggled with over the years have revolved around how I look, my personality flaws, achievement disappointment, inhibitions and fears, a sense of inadequacy and a lack of sense of purpose.

At times, these insecurities can cause me to live in a very self-absorbed way. They frame my life, and colour the way I live. They affect my actions, words and perceptions. They inhibit character transformation because I am trying to protect a part of me that is uncertain and insecure.

There is something in all of us that drives a need to establish that we are loved, that we have a purpose in life, and that we have something meaningful to offer. If we can gain a sense of assurance and security around these basic needs, we will be better equipped to discern what is healthy or unhealthy about ourselves.

Our perception of our value is the starting point for all of this.

Value

A healthy sense of value is vital for good growth. It is needed for establishing equilibrium. It is not healthy to have a prideful estimation of ourselves, and neither is it healthy to think of ourselves as rubbish.

If we tend towards the 'rubbish' estimation of ourselves, we shy away from suggestions of correction because we want to protect ourselves from any further feeling of inadequacy. It can hurt too much. If we already consider ourselves terribly deficient, we don't want any further hurt associated with being told what else is wrong with us! We have already been our own judge and juror, what need have we for any more?

If we tend towards a prideful, overinflated sense of self, we have another sort of barrier in the way of transformation. When we are always 'right', we become unreceptive to correction. We turn off the improvement channel because it is not relevant to us.

God cannot work with us if we are too puffed up in our own estimation. It becomes a form of self-value that puts a hard shell around our hearts that is difficult for God to penetrate. This can also cause us to look down on others with disdain and judgment.

So we want something that might help us find middle ground between the one extreme of 'I'm useless', or the other extreme of 'I'm always right'. I believe that the balance point comes through understanding and receiving God's love.

There is something deeply comforting about feeling loved and valuable. It creates a tenderness in our hearts that allows the barriers and walls of self protection and pride to be lowered. It helps us see how irrelevant some of the things are, that have driven our actions around our self-perception. It helps us become more willing to be vulnerable and open about our fears, inhibitions and weaknesses. It helps to cut us down, or build us up to our rightful size. It establishes a foundation of value that is invaluable to our quest for character transformation.

We will be reminded about how valuable and loved we are in a future chapter. But before we go there, it's worthwhile thinking about some of the unfulfilling ways we try to gain a sense of assurance for ourselves. We frequently establish our own means of self-validation; but as I know from wry experience, it's not a very satisfactory way! Too often I choose a source of validation that is going to stunt the growth of any transformation effort. But there is a better way to establish a sense of assurance, if we will but choose it!

Before we leave this chapter, let's revisit our butterflies. Both butterflies began life as a caterpillar. They came from an egg laid by an adult butterfly. When they emerged from their egg, they were just very tiny caterpillars. They were just a minuscule dot on the leaf of the swan plant. But they had what they needed to grow. The food they would eat in the days to come would enable them to grow and grow and grow …

The foundation for change is set. Each little caterpillar is on the road toward transformation. They are beginning the journey towards something more.

One day, in due course, a process of change will occur. One day a butterfly will be revealed.

In a nutshell:

- We are all on a journey of change from the time of birth until we die.

- The woman who is serious about living life God's way will be intent on transformation.

- Transformation is about choosing to be no longer conformed to the world's way, but to be transformed by the renewing of our minds.

- The transformation journey begins with establishing a foundation of value.

Prayer time:

'Dear Lord, please be with us as we begin a journey of change. Please may we make wise choices in our direction through life. Please help us to trust you in the changes that lie ahead.
You are a mighty God, worthy of all honour and praise. Amen.'

Chapter 2

Comparisonitus

I looked in the mirror, and fell to despair,
What pouchy tired eyes, and distinctly grey hair!
Nose kind of large, and wrinkles defined,
That was only the beginning, what more could I find?

I head to the shops, maybe I'll feel better there,
Perhaps retail therapy can rid my despair.
But time at the shops seems only to make worse,
The me-esteem problem, that's such of a curse!

Now, the lady in front, she helps me feel better,
Compared to her, I'm quite a go-getter!
That fills me with hope – and it's more than a glimmer,
For standing by her, I'm certainly slimmer!

But confidence tumbles, as I look to my right,
The manicured beauty, whose demeanour is bright.
Compared to her, I'm awkward and plain.
Can't I be more like her? is a common refrain.

'Dear Lord', I declare, 'I'm in a bit of a bind.
Can you show me the way, please help me to find,
The right way to see myself, a healthy way to be ...
For I'm struggling, Lord, in accepting me!'

"For you created my inmost being; you knit me together in my mother's womb. I praise you because I am fearfully and wonderfully made; your works are wonderful, I know that full well" (Psalm 139:13,14).

I USED to think my mother had run out of curls to offer by the time I was born. I was number five, in a family of six, and the youngest of the four girls in the family. My three older sisters all had lovely dark brown locks, with varying degrees of wavy to ringlet curly hair.

I always felt rather envious of their hair. Mine was fine, straight and brown. Quite plain and boring, in my view!

Along with 'plain and boring' hair, my features were blessed with a fairly prominent nose and chin. I would look at the lovely proportional noses and chins of some of my peers, and wish that my features had been blessed in a similar way.

My personality has always been reserved. My childhood was shadowed by shyness, sensitivity and a tendency to be a background person. When I started youth group, I felt extremely awed by all the older members. My reserved personality evidently earned me a secret nickname: Miss Parks, because a park is a reserve; and I was reserved. It was years later that I found this out, and by that stage it was rather amusing. But, for the timid insecure teenager I was at the time, all I wanted was to know that I was okay, accepted and wanted.

An inner need for validation and a sense of worth has been with me my whole life.

Value detour

The desire for a sense of worth has an impact on my transformation response. It creates an internal battle within me. I oscillate between a desire to change and improve, and a desire to protect my fragile self-esteem from any crushing blow. I want to be a better person, but frequently I go about it the wrong way.

Your personality is probably very different from mine. Your strengths and fears may be quite unlike mine.

However, as dissimilar as we may be; as different as our insecurities might look, we all have a common need of wanting to be loved and affirmed.

The desire for love, affirmation and purpose can sometimes have us looking in the wrong places. There can be some unhealthy pathways to finding validation. Looking to other people for our sense of worth is often our first port of call. We are greatly influenced by what people think of us; or even what we think they think of us!

Alongside a desire for validation from other people, another issue emerges. Comparison. I call it comparisonitus. Comparisonitus sounds like a disease. In many ways perhaps it is! At any rate, it's a good description of what it's like when comparison runs away with us.

I have found the greatest culprit for my personal insecurities to be comparison. When I feel negative about how I look, it's often because I have compared myself with someone else. Any sense of inadequacy and disappointment with my personality or achievements can all be traced back to comparison. After all, if I have nothing to compare myself to, I would just accept who and what I am because I would know nothing different. But I look to other people for the benchmark of how I should be. The result is always less than ideal.

Comparison can inch its way into all our lives. It's so easy to look over the fence to see the grass looking greener on our neighbour's side!

So how does comparison affect us? Comparison creates an environment in which we analyse how we stack up against others around us. The result is always a lose-lose situation. If the comparison concludes with the feeling that we are above that person in a particular way, then we can be in danger of promoting a smug sense of superiority or self-elevation. If our analysis has us falling short of our comparison subject, then we will feel negative about ourselves, giving us a feeling of inferiority, disappointment or envy. This is all sitting on a foundation that has no solid base. Even if our analysis has us drawing an 'equal straw' with another person, it is still an unsatisfactory means of establishing a sense of worth.

Comparing ourselves with other people means that our sense of value is always shifting. We have no solid foundation. There will always be people who seem superior to us, and there will always be those who seem inferior – in whatever way. Trying to establish a sense of value through comparison gives changeable results, with a roller-coaster effect on our emotions.

Most of the time we don't realise we are making comparisons. It happens so subconsciously. I had no idea how much this was a problem for me, and how it affected me until it was brought to my attention. After that, I began to see it happening regularly. How does my skin, hair or body size compare to the next person? Am I as capable as others? Do I look older or younger than my peers? How 'successful' is my life compared to others? Do I appear to be more, or less confident than the person next to me?

How do I look in that photo compared to everyone else?

It sounds so self-centred and horrible when written like this; but in reality, comparison happens so subconsciously that we barely register that it's happening.

From the time I became aware of how comparison was operating in my life, I began to notice other people using comparison also. I would hear it spoken about on the radio, read of it in articles, or hear it in conversations.

I heard an assertive forthright lady talk about how she used to wish she were more like her quiet, gentle-natured friend. She found out later that this gentle lady had always wished she herself were more like her outgoing friend! They had both been using each other as the measuring standard for ideal personality, and had both come up wanting.

That is what comparison does. It creates a measuring standard that is always moving.

Our word of encouragement one Sunday morning was on the subject of comparison. The speaker gave an excellent talk on the problem that comparison creates. He spoke about how we compare ourselves, our homes, cars, spouses, jobs and children to others. Even our perceived spirituality can be a point of comparison to others. The list of things that we could compare is endless!

He made this statement: 'The fastest way to kill something special is to compare it to something else!' 'Where comparison begins', he concluded, 'contentment ends.'

My husband, Robert, and I were planning a weekend away. We looked on the holiday house sites to choose the ones we liked the look of. We perused all our options and reviewed them with our checklist of things we would like to have in our holiday home.

We had our short list. We had compared prices, facilities, features and what there was to do in each local area. We then made our decision based on all those factors. With excited anticipation, we booked our holiday home. All was ready to go for the date we had arranged. We felt good about our choice. We were happy with what we were getting for what we were paying. But then, for some reason, Robert looked at another holiday home site a few days later. There was the same house that we had just booked, listed for a cheaper rate than what we had just paid. Now he felt disappointed. What had been a good deal before, now felt unsatisfactory. Now it was overpriced and he felt cheated. The exercise in comparison had killed his contentment. Sure, it was still the same place, with all the benefits we had previously valued; but now he felt it was no longer a good deal.

'The fastest way to kill something special is to compare it to something else!'

Dissatisfaction had been initiated, and what we had previously felt was special no longer seemed that way.

Comparison can have a negative impact on how we perceive ourselves. Our deep inner longing is for acceptance, to be wanted, loved and to feel that we have something valuable to offer the world. But comparison causes the bar to move. One day we can feel significant, the next we can feel small and worthless. Usually this is in direct proportion to how we feel we stack up against the person alongside us. There are so many times I have played this scenario out. So many times I have been on the self-esteem emotional roller coaster ride!

My transformation journey has been stunted all too often by unhealthy doses of comparisonitus. Comparison is not a good pathway for development. Healthy 'wings' are not formed by means of comparison!

In the book of Proverbs, Solomon describes one of the effects of comparison:

"A heart at peace gives life to the body, but envy rots the bones" (Proverbs 14:30).

How true that is. Envy, or even superiority, is a very unfulfilling way of establishing a sense of worth.

Stars and dots

It can be all too easy to use other people to gauge our worth. It's a very natural thing to do. People's perspectives, views and opinions are always important to us. We want to know that they think we are okay. Their successes seem like something desirable to work towards ourselves. When their words or actions seem to indicate that they don't think very highly of us, it can be crushing. Our sense of worth can come crashing right down. When we can't seem to replicate their success, we feel inferior or envious. Our sense of worth is greatly impacted by what other people think.

Much as we will always need some sort of affirmation by the significant people in our lives, it can't be our main source of assurance. It has limitations. Relying on it has potential for great disappointment. Sometimes assurance is poorly, or even negatively, expressed. Sometimes affirmation never comes, even when we are desperately wanting it!

Validation from other people needs to be kept in perspective.

So, if establishing a sense of value and worth is not ultimately going to be found through the means of other people, what is our foundation?

I love the story of Punchinello.

Punchinello is a children's storybook character. He is a little wooden Wemmick, who lives in a town with other wooden Wemmicks. All the Wemmicks have been fashioned by the wood carver who lives on top of the hill, called Eli.

The Wemmicks spend their time giving each other rewards, of stars or dots. They give out stars when a Wemmick is talented, clever and good looking. They give out dots when a Wemmick has chipped paint, does something stupid, or is just an average sort of Wemmick.

Punchinello seemed to have a talent for being given dots. His paint was often chipped, he would make mistakes, and he didn't seem to have any clever abilities. He was covered in dots, given to him by his fellow Wemmicks.

Punchinello believed that he was just no good, and would never be able to do anything that was star worthy!

Then one day he came across a girl Wemmick who had neither stars nor dots on her. He asked her why she didn't have any stars or dots. 'Oh', she said, 'They won't stick to me. I go up the hill every day to spend time with the wood carver, Eli. I find that spending time with him stops the stars or dots from sticking to me. If a fellow Wemmick tries to give me a star, it won't stick. If they try to give me a dot, it won't stick. Eli helps me understand how special I am without the need of stars or dots!'

That sounded pretty good to Punchinello, who decided that he too would pay a visit to the wood carver up the hill.

Eli had been waiting for him. 'I wondered when you would come to see me, Punchinello!'

With the help of Eli, Punchinello came to realise that he didn't need stars or dots to dictate his worth. Eli had fashioned and made him. He was special because he was made by a master craftsman. 'And', Eli concluded emphatically, 'I don't make mistakes!'

What a beautiful illustration of finding worth.[1]

Our ultimate value comes from God. He is our heavenly Father, who has formed and fashioned us as we are. He is the Master Craftsman. Our unique features and personalities are His gift to us. He wants us to be able to take the raw material He has gifted us with, and allow Him to grow and fashion something really beautiful out of it. He wants us to know that we are wanted and loved. He has gone to such lengths to show us what we are worth to Him. It is through Him, and the work of our Lord Jesus, that our most solid foundation of value comes.

The Lord Jesus is the one person who managed to maintain a sense of purpose and value in the face of complete rejection and desertion by all others. The terrible slurs on his

---

[1]   *You are Special*, by Max Luccado.

character, mission and authority by the leaders of the people would have hurt. The lack of support from his followers right at the end must have dealt him a hard blow. Even his own family, it seemed, had doubts about his sanity! How alone he would have felt. Despised and rejected by men. Oppressed and afflicted. All of this rejection and lack of affirmation could have been crippling for him. He could have given up on his purpose, and walked away from his mission. Such an overwhelming amount of dots!

But Jesus' strong sense of purpose, and knowledge of his value was instilled so deeply into him by his heavenly Father, that it helped keep him on track. No amount of ridicule, persecution, disbelief, cruel words or slander could keep him from fulfilling all that was intended for him. The 'dots' couldn't stick. The 'stars' didn't stick either. Not in a way that might have turned his head with a sense of pride. There was only One that he wanted to please.

Jesus' strength, purpose and value came from his loving Father, who had his back the whole way.

It was this that gave him the power and ability to achieve all that he did.

I don't know about you, but that is what I would like to aspire to. I would like to be able to get to the point where 'stars' or 'dots' can't stick to me, particularly in a way that forms any negative reaction. I want to get to the point where time spent with the Master Craftsman builds up in me a healthy sense of value and love. I want to get to the point where I can value both myself – and others – as somebody unique and special. I would love to live without need for unhealthy comparisonitus.

In our next chapter we will expand further on God's great love and the value He places on us.

Meanwhile, we have much to think about. Let's ask ourselves these questions:

- 'Am I okay in my own skin?'
- 'Where is my sense of value coming from?'
- 'How much is comparison affecting my life?'
- 'How much am I relying on validation from other people for my sense of worth?'

We all want and need a sense of value. We want to know we are wanted and loved. Sometimes this desire takes us down the roundabout route of comparison, or of being reliant on validation from other people. Can we find a more satisfactory means of worth? I believe we can.

In the next chapter we will immerse ourselves in the security and value offered us through God's great love for us. We are a special and unique creation!

In a nutshell:

- Our deep inner longing is to know that we are okay, wanted and loved.
- Validation from people is often the way we look for a sense of worth. Comparison is a major factor in this.
- The fastest way to kill something special is to compare it to something else.
- Time spent with his heavenly Father gave Jesus a strong sense of value. On the strength of that, he could go on living out the fullness of his purpose, without being reliant on the validation he might have had from others.
- God's love creates value in us.

Prayer time:

'Our Father, thank you for the life you have given to us! Thank you for making us as we are. But sometimes, Lord, we struggle to accept what you have made, and we compare ourselves to your other children. Please help us to see the value you have created in each of us, without feeling the need to compare it to someone else. Please help us to see that we lose satisfaction and contentment in what you have given us, when we look at what others have!

Thank you for what you have given to us, and how you have made us, Lord. Amen.'

And the Father looked down from His throne on High,
He said, 'Come to me child, come and draw nigh.
I will show you your worth, way beyond compare,
Child, don't look to others, don't fall to despair.'

Chapter 3

Unique and special

He showed me a garden, perfect and new,
A man and woman within, the only two.
'Look closely', He said, 'If only you could tell,
You too, like them, I've made "wonderfully well"!'

"So God created man in his own image, in the image of God he created him; male and female he created them" (Genesis 1:27, ESV).

"God saw all that he had made, and it was very good" (verse 31).

"In him we were also chosen, having been predestined according to the plan of him who works out everything in conformity with the purpose of his will, in order that we, who were the first to hope in Christ, might be for the praise of his glory" (Ephesians 1:11,12).

THE swan plant was teeming with new life. Our two caterpillars were a part of that new life. They were not alone. Many other little caterpillars had emerged from their egg sacks, and were eager to eat. The swan plant leaves were their nourishment and life food. This was their way to grow larger and stronger. They would keep eating and growing until the time they would eventually be big enough, and ready, for transformational change.

Lots of new little creatures. Each one made in the image of its kind. Each with a life of growth and change ahead of it. Each equipped with the potential to become something more and different.

Caterpillars are all made very similar. It's difficult to tell one caterpillar apart from another. They all have the same colours, shape and features that define their particular variety.

We humans are a little different. While we all have roughly the same form as each other, there are distinct differences within that framework. Physical differences. Personality differences. We are each individual and unique.

But we are all the same in this way: we are all made by a Master Designer, and we are made "fearfully and wonderfully" well.

David penned a few beautiful verses celebrating, and praising God, for the life and body he had been given:

"For you created my inmost being; you knit me together in my mother's womb. I praise you because I am fearfully and wonderfully made; your works are wonderful, I know that full well. My frame was not hidden from you when I was made in the secret place, when I was woven together in the depths of the earth. Your eyes saw my unformed body; all the days ordained for me were written in your book before one of them came to be" (Psalm 139:13-16).

As well as being made fearfully and wonderfully well, we have been gifted with something very special. We have been made in the image of Elohim – Mighty Ones.

Genesis 1:27 puts it this way:

"So God created man in his own image, in the image of God he created him; male and female he created them" (ESV).

This is something that should fill us with great awe. We are made in the image of God.

"God saw all that he had made, and it was very good" (verse 31).

Adam and Eve were the first people to be made in this way. Adam was given the honoured title of being "son of God" (see Luke 3:38).

For better (and for worse), we are children of Adam. We have the same heritage.

What a privilege it is to be considered a son or daughter of God.

Chosen

Robert has a childhood story about not being chosen. Robert was born with a number of medical issues. This included having a short leg and a club foot. Sports games at school were difficult for him. He could not run fast, and he frequently got puffed out, due to asthma. This put him at a disadvantage. It also made him an unappealing choice of team mate. He recalls standing in the line up of children waiting to be chosen for a team. The leader of each team would call a child's name to join their team, until all children were allocated. Invariably, Robert would be the last child to be picked. It was out of a sense of obligation that the last team leader would call Robert's name to join their group.

If you have ever experienced the humiliation of being the last one, the unwanted one, you will know what this feels like. You are the leftover. You are the one that would be discarded if the teams were allowed to do so. You are regarded as the weak link in their group; the one who is most likely to let them down.

It's not just childhood sports games that can become the platform for rejection. Perhaps there are moments when we feel unwanted, unlovable, awkward, the odd one out, different, misunderstood, untalented, unbeautiful ...

Maybe many of us have encountered such moments, when we just wished we could be a chosen one! The times where we would like to shine in an outstanding way. To stand out in the crowd.

The beautiful thing about the value that God bestows, is that we are chosen by Him. Being chosen by God does not mean that somebody else misses out. It does not mean that we will outshine others. Being chosen by God means we will not be the one who is left at 'the end of the line', who is grudgingly allowed to be a part of the group. Nobody is left out; for all are offered the opportunity to be a part of God's family. We are invited to become one of His team. That is what is so unique and special about being God-chosen. He wants us, and He loves us. We are made in the image of Elohim. We are each made individual and unique; each one gifted with talent that gives life meaning and purpose.

The love that God shows to us is one that bestows value, despite it not being either deserved or earned by us. He wants us to have a relationship with Him, like a Father and a child. He wants us to trust Him, spend time with Him, obey Him, delight in Him, believe Him, and live out purpose-filled lives for Him.

His love is our most secure form of value. Value is not found in what other people think of us. It's not found in our comparison with other people. It is ultimately found in what God thinks of us.

God's love shows us that we are wanted; not because we are clever, talented, good looking or even good. He loves us because we are His children, and He has invested so much into us.

Valuable

Robert had a few favourite teddy bears when he was a child. They were cuddled, taken to bed with him, dragged outside, and generally loved to raggedness. They had a special place in his heart. So much so, that several of them made their way into our home after we got married, long after Robert had outgrown them. They became a part of our own children's lives.

By the time Sink, the teddy bear, arrived at our house, his blue overalls were very faded. Loose threads were evident, and his little white face was very dirty! But our own children still loved him, despite all of this. He is still at our house. Nobody has the heart to throw him out. He would not be considered valuable in a monetary way. He would not even be considered desirable. But he has a value of a sort. It is the value that is given by love. There is sentimentality attached to this teddy bear because, once upon a time, love was invested into him by a small child who treasured him.

Love, pictured in this way, is similar to how we might view God's love for us. We are valuable to Him because He has invested so much love into us. God has proved His love over and over again. Just in case we have trouble really believing that we could be considered valuable, let's remind ourselves of some verses from God's Word.

On a basic level, God's love extends to all His creation. In His goodness, He allows both the good and the evil to receive the blessing of rain and sun; and then the blessings that flow on from that.

"... He causes his sun to rise on the evil and the good, and sends rain on the righteous and the unrighteous" (Matthew 5:45).

"Look at the birds of the air; they do not sow or reap or store away in barns, and yet your heavenly Father feeds them. Are you not more valuable than they?" (Matthew 6:26).

"Are not five sparrows sold for two pennies? Yet not one of them is forgotten by God. Indeed, the very hairs of your head are all numbered. Don't be afraid; you are worth more than many sparrows" (Luke 12:6,7).

"For God so loved the world that he gave his one and only Son, that whoever believes in him shall not perish but have eternal life" (John 3:16).

"But God demonstrates his own love for us in this: While we were still sinners, Christ died for us" (Romans 5:8).

On a deeper level, God's love extends to forgiveness, grace and eternal life – if we accept it and respond to it.

"This is how God showed his love among us: He sent his one and only Son into the world that we might live through him. This is love: not that we loved God, but that he loved us and sent his Son as an atoning sacrifice for our sins" (1 John 4:9,10).

"But because of his great love for us, God, who is rich in mercy, made us alive with Christ even when we were dead in transgressions – it is by grace you have been saved" (Ephesians 2:4,5).

"Blessed are those whose transgressions are forgiven, whose sins are covered. Blessed is the one whose sin the Lord will never count against them" (Romans 4:7,8).

"Do not be afraid, little flock, for your Father has been pleased to give you the kingdom" (Luke 12:32).

Look at what lengths the Father has gone to, to show us His love. With love, God fashioned and formed us, giving us life, personality, feature and form. He gave us choice, hope and purpose. He provided food to eat, and everything else we need to thrive and grow. He offered us a life of fellowship with Him. And if this was not enough, when sin entered the world, and man was separated from God because of it, God sent us His perfect Son.

The obedient Son, the 'second Adam', was prepared to lay down his life for the flawed sons of Adam, so that we might understand the depth of love our Father has for us. All this so that we could have restored fellowship.

Even more, He has offered us everlasting life so that we can have eternal fellowship and a loving relationship with Him.

God is the author of love. Without His love, we would have no idea what love really is. His is a true, deep and sacrificing love.

None of this is because we deserve it. We let Him down time and time again. We have ragged edges, and are dirty because of sin. Yet, out of compassion and love for His creation, God pours out His love on us.

God's love shows us that we are valuable, loved and wanted. He has invested so much into showing us His love. If we can recognise it, and see it, then God's love for us will become the foundation of our value.

God's love bestows value, despite our unworthiness. Our human love gauges value, and then rewards it according to our assessment of worth. What a difference. I think it is definitely worth spending time immersed in the truth of God's love, and the value it bestows!

It will help us believe it and see it.

There are times when I am in need of some well grounded perspective. I experience doubt, self-pity, worry or unhappiness. I feel inadequate, and perhaps unlovable. I have learnt to take these moments to the foot of the cross.

In my imagination, I have looked into the pain-filled face of my dear Lord. Much as I would like to avoid observing the blood running down his brow, or the bleeding wounds on his body, it is necessary. It is necessary to raise my eyes to his eyes. His eyes are dulled by pain, but they are willing to make contact with mine. I imagine myself speaking my words of complaint, inadequacy, woe or discontent. I imagine telling him I'm unlovable, untalented or not good enough. And I find that the words won't come out. They dry on my lips. Could I ever dare to express feelings of self-pity, dissatisfaction, or unhappiness in the face of such love? Somehow, whatever I feel woeful about is nothing compared to the love shown in this single act of sacrifice.

As I linger in that place, I continue to imagine my problem, pain, sin or inadequacy nailed up on that cross with my Lord. I remind myself that he took my pain, he bore my burdens. He was pierced for my transgressions, and was crushed for my iniquities. And I remind myself that 'the punishment that brought me peace was on him, and by his wounds I am healed'. Finally, in my imagination, I fast forward to the end of the crucifixion story. I see a cross, no longer in use. It is lying on the ground, empty of its occupant. As I look closer, all I can see on that cross is blood stains. They are the silent witness to the horror of death that had been enacted on this piece of wood. But wait, there is more. As I look, I imagine words written in the blood. My words of burden are there. Whatever sin, whatever sense of inadequacy, whatever fear or pain; it is written there in the blood. As I watch, I see those words overlaid by other words: 'This is how much you are loved!'

This exercise is one of the most powerful, humbling experiences I have ever engaged in. It leaves me in no doubt of how much my heavenly Father and my Lord Jesus love me, and to what extent they have gone to show it.

Thanks be to God for His great love – that is shown us especially through the sacrifice of His dear Son!

Valuable, loved and wanted? Definitely. Precious, unique and special? Most certainly.

Our worth cannot be compared with others, because it is individual and unique to ourselves. If we can see and believe in God's love, we will start to see a new perspective about our value.

The positive words of love and purpose that are written in God's precious Word are special. If we believe them, and let them fill us, we will find the assurance that we all need: that we are wanted, loved and valuable.

"Dearly loved", "Valuable", "Worth more than ...", "Forgiven", "Washed clean", "Saved by grace", "Child of God", "Growing" "Chosen" ...

God's love bestows value, despite us not deserving it. There is nothing in us that is of itself valuable. We cannot earn it. But God has invested so much into His flawed little children. He isn't giving up on us. We are worth the blood of His precious Son. This is life-changing, if we can only believe it. If we receive it and respond to it, it will become our foundation for spiritual transformation. The love and purpose God has shown us is the structure by which we can now grow the investment God has made in us. We have a responsibility to create value through our lives, by what God has given to us. We have an exciting – and challenging – journey of growth ahead of us!

Caterpillars are made in the image of caterpillars. We are made in the image of Elohim, formed and created with the purpose of being like our Lord. How awe-inspiring this is. What a privilege. We are special and unique, because we are designed by a loving God. We are loved and chosen. Not because we deserve it, but because God's great sacrificing love made it possible.

"See what great love the Father has lavished on us, that we should be called children of God! And that is what we are!" (1 John 3:1).

A child of God. Valued. What a special and wonderful privilege!

In a nutshell:

- Mankind has such a privileged position in God's creation. Created and called to be a child of God.

- God's love bestows value on us, even though we don't deserve it. Human love gauges value, and rewards it according to assessment of worth.

- God's love is the foundation of our value.

- Receiving God's love is the foundation for future growth.

Prayer time:

'Dear Lord, thank you for the privilege of being known as a "child of God". This comes from your great love which you have lavished on us. Please may we believe this love that you have for us. Please may we learn to see it in every area of our lives. Amen.'

Chapter 4

Enhancing value

"Do you not know that your bodies are temples of the Holy Spirit ...? You are not your own; you were bought at a price. Therefore honour God with your bodies" (1 Corinthians 6:19,20).

"Be still, and know that I am God" (Psalm 46:10).

"Therefore, as we have opportunity, let us do good to all people, especially to those who belong to the family of believers" (Galatians 6:10).

A LOVE that bestows value, as God has done for us, deserves a response. In fact, it creates responsibility. For it to be truly received in our lives, it requires some action on our part. We need to believe it and respond to it. God's love is limited to our response and reception of it.

Responding to God's love

The exciting – and challenging – part is that the value that has been bestowed on us has further potential. It invites growth. God expects growth.

In butterfly terms, it means that the caterpillar will first accept that it's a caterpillar. But it doesn't have to stay a caterpillar. It is designed to grow and change. Something even better lies ahead.

One of the ways we enhance value in our lives, is to look after the natural body we have been gifted with. Our bodies are a 'temple' of God's spirit, and deserve respectful handling.

In this chapter we will consider a few ways in which we can enhance our sense of value and appreciation for our natural bodies. We will consider how we can begin to build value in our lives.

We have been made individual and unique. We are all a daughter of God, but with individual features and personalities. Each of us will have slightly different ways in which we may create value in our lives, but we do all have something to offer!

Smile

One of the best ways we can enhance our natural beauty and transform our face is to smile ... lots. This is a completely natural and inexpensive beauty tip; and great for enhancing our facial features.

Robert regularly used to encounter a woman out jogging, while he was cycling on his way to work. Her features at a glance were very plain. But as they passed each other along the way, she would look up with a huge smile on her face, and give him an enthusiastic 'Good morning!' Her whole face would light up, and one that could only ordinarily be described as plain became beautiful. The ordinary features became extraordinary! He used to go on his way feeling uplifted and encouraged. That smile made his day.

This lady had the secret of beauty within easy grasp, and she used it to great effect! Her smile gave her beauty.

Smiling does a lot for us. It not only transforms our face, it creates a sense of well-being. It can make a world of difference, not only to our external features, but to our fragile self esteem. It can also make a big difference to someone else's day! A smile that lifts our mouth and lights up our face and eyes, is an infectious thing indeed. Simple but beautiful.

Look after your body

It's an old cliché, but it's true: what you don't use, you lose. I know! My stomach muscles, which have been extended beyond their normal limits four times over through pregnancy, have completely lost their original tone. Now everything down that direction resembles jelly far more than muscle. It's going to take some effort to change that scenario!

Keeping our bodies healthy and better toned requires regular exercise. It will do our body a big favour. Exercise also raises positive endorphins. Starting with something that we enjoy is probably the most palatable way to begin, if we haven't already established exercise in our daily life.

I remember the first time in many years that I tried riding a bicycle. I huffed and puffed my way up the hill on our street, and decided I would call it a day. However, having had some more cycling time since the original hill ride, I have developed more stamina and my enjoyment of it has increased substantially.

Eating healthy food is also beneficial. What we choose to eat affects what our bodies become.

To enhance value in our natural bodies, we need to look after them. This will also include taking time to rest and be still.

Robert and I both know how easy it is to destroy balance in our bodies by constant doing, and ignoring the need to rest. Robert experienced burn-out a while ago, and seven years on he is still experiencing the effects of it. Too much 'doing' made his body decide it had had enough, and the symptoms of burn-out began. After that, his body forced him to rest, but it was not a pleasant way to go about it!

The issue for me has been one of rush. I'm constantly in a rush. I fail to enjoy the journey because my mind is always onto the next thing. I leave myself with very little margin in my life, and it causes stress, frustration and impatience.

Rest and stillness are a necessary part of our relationship with God.

"Be still, and know that I am God", Psalm 46:10 tells us.

"In repentance and rest is your salvation, in quietness and trust is your strength" (Isaiah 30:15).

It is important for the health of our bodies to take time to breathe, to refresh and enjoy the journey along life's pathway.

There is also scope for the enhancement of our physical looks. For most of us, this is an area of our lives that already receives a reasonable amount of attention! Let's keep beauty enhancement simple. Stay sympathetic towards your natural beauty. External extras don't need to be that which defines us. Under any make-up, hair colour or clothing fashion that we may choose to apply, must still be our own unique selves, shining brightly. Remember that God's favourite fashion accessory for us is not that of 'outward adornment', but rather a 'gentle and quiet inner spirit'. That's worth a lot to God, and it is the 'make up' He most appreciates us applying (see 1 Peter 3:3,4).

Individual and unique

I had a refreshing conversation with a young man at a youth gathering. He has an exuberant appreciation of his own unique character. Matthew told me that he was afraid of getting older, and gaining more responsibilities. He confided, 'Responsibility will make me lose my insanity!' 'Insanity?' I questioned.

'I don't want to be like everyone else' he asserted. 'My insanity is a part of who I am!'

He went on to tell me that his stepfather was always the same: monotone. 'I don't ever want to become monotone!' he told me very emphatically. Somehow, I don't think he will. Not if he can maintain his current enthusiastic approach to his unique different-ness. If he can resist the urge to follow the crowd, or conform to a pattern of sameness, he will remain an individual with a lot of character!

Appreciating our own individual personalities is something for us all to aspire to. God has made us all so different. We can celebrate our own unique qualities, alongside appreciating the unique qualities of the next person. Different doesn't mean wrong!

Being comfortable with who we are does have some limitations, however. Bad, unhealthy, lazy or God-displeasing behaviours are not something we should tolerate in ourselves. Excusing any of these on the grounds of 'well that is just who I am, people can like it or lump it!' is not okay. There are certain boundaries around our acceptance of who we are. Our behaviour should be examined in the light of whether it is healthy, wise and God honouring. God does expect us to exercise our individual traits sensitively and responsibly.

I have been blessed with a very vivid imagination. It is part of who I am. This has been very useful in my Sunday School teaching years, with helping Bible stories come alive. But more frequently I use my vivid imagination to imagine all sorts of terrible possible disasters and worse-case scenarios that could happen in any given situation. This is an unhealthy behaviour, and a very untrusting thing to do! It is something I need to address and modify.

We can work with our personalities in a way that helps us to grow. Rough edges can be refined. Bad habits can be redirected to become positive habits. Behaviour can be modified. Let us follow the examples from others in the areas that we appreciate about them. What we observe about other people, with their positive characteristics, can be helpful. We can weave those positive characteristics into our own lives, and learn from them. But let's not try to be that person.

We are still uniquely us with our own individual personalities.

Feed the soul

'What goes in is what comes out.' Let's be careful about what we feed our minds. Reading material that is positive and wholesome is the best choice for enhancing value for our minds. We want words that build up and promote peace, rather than unrest or dissatisfaction. The same goes for what we watch; at the movies, on television, Netflix, or on the internet.

Negative self-talk can also become an issue. When we nurture dissatisfaction, or when we find ourselves rehearsing any hurt brought about by what others may say or think of us.

I know how easy it is to feel crushed by criticism. Frequently my mind resembles a compact disc on replay. It plays negative thoughts that swirl round and round with nauseating repetitiveness. These thoughts need to be captured, cut off, and replaced with positive ones.

Let us keep reminding ourselves of the positive truthful words of value that God has given us.

Watch out for what I call the 'grey attitude'. As I got older, my hair became quite grey. I hated it, and felt quite negative about myself because of it. I used to think: 'It makes me look so old ...'! Because Robert preferred me not to use hair colour, I didn't; but I was most unhappy about how I looked. My attitude was greyer than my hair! From this issue, I came up with a phrase that has made a big difference to me: 'A grey attitude is much worse than grey hair.' Now, whenever I start to feel negative about myself again, I say: 'Grey hair is better than a grey attitude!' I'll take grey hair over a grey attitude any day!

Pray and meditate

To keep growing in a positive and healthy way, let us make time to spend with God. We can tell Him our fears and inhibitions. We can tell Him our doubts and worries. We can tell Him our needs and desires. We can listen to His positive reassurances. He will speak to us through His Word, and through the "still small voice" of peace in our minds. Let us remember that He made us as we are. He has a plan and purpose for us.

For years I struggled with insomnia. It became so bad, that I was getting stressed about even going to bed. I would have panic attacks many nights because I couldn't get to sleep. At about the time when I thought I would need to start taking anti-depressants to try and combat the emotional mess I was in, I heard a talk that addressed the power of prayer and meditation. The speaker said, 'Prayer and meditation does for the brain what exercise does for the body'. I started on a more regular daily prayer routine, rather than just the 'snack' type of prayer that I had done before. I noticed positive changes to my poor sleeping habits within the first week! Prayer also became a useful tool for calming my mind during panicky sleepless moments.

Prayer is a soothing balm for the clamour that goes on in our minds!

Like prayer, meditation on God's Word is highly beneficial. It gives us our anchor point for life and truth. Allowing the words, principles and concepts from God's Word to swirl round our minds, and sink deeply into our hearts is a life-changer. It is a sure and firm foundation for us. When we read God's Word, we receive information. When we meditate on God's Word, we open our hearts to transformation. And that is certainly what we are aiming for!

Looking outside ourselves

One of the biggest ways we can enhance value is to live for something bigger than ourselves. When we are wrapped up only in ourselves, we make a very small package! Reaching out to others is a great value enhancing experience.

Try some Random Acts of Kindness. We could take on a project that takes the focus off ourselves and on to something else. Anything that helps take the focus off ourselves and puts it on to someone or something else, will really help us grow.

In our previous home we lived in a low socio-economic area. I was incredibly impressed, when a family chose to come and live in our street, specifically to minister there. They saw an opportunity to witness about God and live a life of service in our area. I came to know Joanne, the mum of the family. I saw how she got involved in the Bible in Schools programme; she started a 'Mums In Touch' prayer group to pray for our local school, the teachers and children; she also got involved in helping run a Girls Rally at the local community centre. The whole family were active with their outreach, and living for something that was 'bigger than themselves'. We could see what a joy it was to them to be able to reach out to others.

We too will benefit and grow immensely from finding ways to look outside of ourselves. The joy achieved from living for something bigger than ourselves turns it into a rewarding exercise!

Value foundation

It's useful to keep reminding ourselves of where value begins:

- The foundation of our value begins with God. His love bestows value, even though we do not deserve it.

- God's unfailing love is shown us through our Lord Jesus' sacrifice.

- Words of value and love are written to us in God's Word, they become our assurance and anchor point.

- Our value is in who He is, not in who we are. Our strength, purpose and significance are in Him.

- Our value does not come from what we look like – our outward appearance is changeable and fickle.

- Our value does not come from what we do – although what we do can influence what we become.

- Our value is not defined in what other people say about us – especially the negative words. Neither is it in the negative self-talk that we might tell ourselves.

There is great value in accepting and recognising the love that God has poured into our lives.

May God's love become the foundation on which our value begins.

As we conclude this chapter, let's just take a look in on our caterpillars. Life on the swan plant is going well.

The small caterpillars are eating and growing. Their little bodies are getting bigger with all the goodness they have been putting into them. Each day they look a little different. Changing. The growth is healthy and good. It's so good to see these little creatures growing, nourished by the food that will help them become what they were designed to be.

But there are some dangers out there. There are problems that could stunt the ability to grow. There are pests that can kill.

There are things to beware of ...

In a nutshell:

- Our value begins with God's love.

- Looking after our natural bodies honours the One who made them. Our bodies should be treated with respect.

- Smile!

- The disciplines of prayer and meditation on God's word help keep us anchored and balanced.

- Reaching out to others, and living for something bigger than ourselves, are some of the biggest ways we can build value in our lives.

Prayer time:

Let us pray each day for the ability and know-how to look after our bodies in a way that honours God. Let us pray that God will open our hearts to be able to give of ourselves, and to live for something bigger than ourselves. Amen.

Chapter 5

A thankful heart

I paused to reflect on what I was learning –
Confidence in God's love is what I'm discerning.
Accepting how He has made me to be,
Without need to compare, for He's uniquely made me!

I realised how ungrateful to Him I must seem,
A thankful heart I must grow, if I want to redeem
Lost time and perspective – a new way to see,
With God's view as my focus – a right way to be.

"... always giving thanks to God the Father for everything, in the name of our Lord Jesus Christ" (Ephesians 5:20).

"Shout for joy to the LORD, all the earth. Worship the LORD with gladness; come before him with joyful songs. Know that the LORD is God. It is he who made us, and we are his; we are his people, the sheep of his pasture. Enter his gates with thanksgiving and his courts with praise; give thanks to him and praise his name" (Psalm 100:1-4).

CATERPILLARS don't have a great deal of choice as to how life goes for them. They hatch, they eat, they grow. They are on a pathway towards transformation that should all go smoothly if they don't encounter any difficulties!

Sadly, life is never that straightforward, and a small caterpillar often encounters challenges.

One of the pests a caterpillar might encounter in its lifetime are wasps. Wasps love to eat caterpillars. Given a chance, they will suck the life out of a small defenceless caterpillar. We have lost many caterpillars at our place to these pests.

One way that caterpillars and butterflies can be protected from pests is in a butterfly house. A butterfly house is a large enclosure that is designed to keep butterflies in, and predators out. They protect the life that's inside from the harm that is outside.

I have visited a few butterfly houses over the years. It is so delightful to go into these places to see the myriads of butterflies that live freely within, protected from any pests that might be out there to destroy them.

These butterfly houses are a little haven of protection for the beautiful little creatures inside.

In our previous chapter, we considered some of the ways that we can enhance value in our natural bodies, and how looking outside of ourselves gives us a positive outward focus.

In this chapter, we will look at one of greatest practices that we have available to help keep us protected from some of the pests in our lives that want to rob us of life.

In addition to protection, this discipline is another worthwhile value enhancing practice.

What am I referring to when I talk of 'life robbers'? No, it's not wasps, but these pests can have similar results!

We've already encountered one of the pests: comparison. But there are other companion pests that can rob us of living fully and freely.

Dissatisfaction, self-pity, resentment, envy, coveting, complaining, inferiority, superiority, arrogance, ego ...

Anything, really, that pulls us down, or puffs us up. Like the butterflies that are protected from negative influences by the butterfly house, we also want something that can provide us with a protective haven.

The protective discipline I am referring to is thankfulness. It is not a magic cure-all formula, but it goes a long way towards giving us balance and perspective. It is a helpful repellent to the nasty pests that want to dominate our lives.

For thankfulness to have the best effect, we will need to cultivate it thoroughly, so that it becomes a natural feature of our lives.

With effort, and with God's help, we will find that thankfulness can become a wall of protection from those things that would rob us of life.

God's instruction

Giving thanks, and being thankful, are practices that God wants us to engage in. We know this is true because we are told to give thanks plenty of times throughout scripture. Here are a few of them:

"Always giving thanks to God the Father for everything, in the name of our Lord Jesus Christ" (Ephesians 5:20).

"Let the peace of Christ rule in your hearts, since as members of one body you were called to peace. And be thankful" (Colossians 3:15).

"Devote yourselves to prayer, being watchful and thankful" (4:2).

"So then, just as you received Christ Jesus as Lord, continue to live in him ... overflowing with thankfulness" (2:6,7).

There are many more places. These verses are just a small sample.

Psalm 100 is a psalm that has the caption "For giving thanks". It is a psalm that has giving thanks and praise inextricably linked to God and His goodness the whole way through.

If God has so much instruction in His Word regarding being thankful, and expressing thankfulness, then it must be a significant thing to act on.

At a basic level, expressing thanks to God is a common courtesy. Just as we would say thank you to the people who have given, or done something for us, so it is important to say thank you to God. God has supplied all we need for life, hope and forgiveness. We owe Him our very lives. This is an extremely thankworthy thing!

In addition to thankfulness being God honouring, it does incredible things for our own psyche. It creates a repelling barrier to the nasty pests that frequently want to dominate us. Grumbling cannot live in the same space as a heartfelt expression of thankfulness! They are polar opposites.

Even if nasty pests are not particularly a problem for us, cultivating thankfulness will enhance our lives and will give us reason to smile.

Benefits of thankfulness

I remember one morning that I was feeling in a particularly low mood. Life was feeling overwhelming. I had been struggling with sleep, problems seemed large, and I felt like I was wading through treacle. I felt heavy and lethargic in my body, and my mind was a bleak churning whirlpool.

This particular morning, I decided to devote my whole prayer time, while out walking, to expressions of thankfulness. I spoke thankfulness – out loud – for everything I could think of.

The beautiful flowers along the way. The green of the trees and the grass. Food to eat, a home to live in, a wonderful husband and family, an amazing God ...!

When I had exhausted my own supply of thankful ideas, I asked God to show me more. With my mind open to further possibilities, I was able to fill the entire walk with wonderful thank-filled thoughts and expression.

How did I feel at the end of that walk? Nothing like how I was when I first started! By the end of that walk, I felt lighter in my heart, body and spirit. Maybe nothing had physically changed about my original situation, but my psyche had. My attitude had been changed considerably, and it made a huge difference to how I now viewed my world.

Research has linked gratitude with an increase in self-esteem, resiliency, better sleep, improved physical health and overall life satisfaction. It builds a positive mindset. Growing a thankful attitude helps us adjust the lens through which we view the world. Happiness and satisfaction are not determined so much by the external world, as by the way we view the external world. What we focus on becomes our reality. What we focus on helps create our character.

Thankfulness has great benefits to our mind and health. My own experience with thankfulness meditation has helped me appreciate the change in attitude that it brings.

Growing thankfulness will help us in a number of ways. It expresses gratitude for what we have, and for what God is doing in our lives. It helps provide a protective barrier around our hearts to ward off the pests. It is a life enhancing practice. It aids healthy character growth. It has physical and mental benefits.

With all these advantages, it's easy to see that thankfulness is a very valuable discipline to have in our lives!

That leads us on to the next thought: thankfulness needs to be cultivated and used regularly to allow it to be the protective shield that we want it to be.

An opposite reaction

If expressing thanks was always a natural reaction, then we would think that someone who was healed of a dreadful life-threatening illness would be the first to express their gratitude. There were ten men in this situation who had a life-restoring encounter with the Lord Jesus.

These ten men had leprosy. They had come to Jesus, begging to be healed. Jesus responded with compassion, and ministered to their need, by instructing them to go and show themselves to the Priest. The men obeyed the instruction, and along the way, they received healing from their deadly illness.

Of the ten men healed, only one man came back to Jesus to say thank you, and to praise God.

"Were there not ten healed? Where are the other nine?"

Taking things for granted can be all too easy. We take it for granted that when we turn on a tap, water will come out. We take for granted that when we turn the light switch on, there will be light. It's only when something goes wrong with these things that we give it any thought.

I had a dear friend who used to say that she gave thanks for water every day when she took a shower. There was no taking warm water for granted with her!

One speaker at a Bible Class posed the question: 'Who prayed for a safe journey out to the class tonight?' No takers. He then asked: 'Who gave thanks for their safe arrival?' No one put up their hand.

Sadly, there are so many things we take for granted.

Growing a gratitude response may take a bit of training – especially for those of us who might tend towards a 'glass half empty' personality.

Even for those who have a naturally bright, bubbly, positive personality, thankfulness 'workouts' are a useful discipline.

We will consider some of the practical ways that we can help train ourselves towards an attitude of gratitude in the next chapter.

Meanwhile, I would like to introduce you to the idea of an 'opposite reaction'.

One of Newton's laws of physics says: "For every action, there is an equal but opposite reaction." This is a concept that can be applied to gratitude. While the equal but opposite reaction of physics will happen naturally without manipulation, the reaction of gratitude in the face of negative feelings is not such a natural thing. Negative feelings need some help for them to swing the opposite way.

Thankfulness cannot coexist with grumbling or dissatisfaction. So, every time we find a negative attitude or thought arising, we need to give it the Opposite Reaction Treatment!

I love the story of Corrie and Betsy Ten Boom. This is the true story of two sisters who were imprisoned in a Nazi concentration camp for hiding Jews in their home in Holland during the Second World War. This particular incident highlights how the practice of thankfulness in this terrible place gave them incredible blessing.

Their time in the camp was horrific. We who have never experienced anything of the sort would find it hard to comprehend. So much suffering, so much misery.

The two sisters were assigned to a barrack that caused them horror and disgust. The place reeked badly, was severely overcrowded, and their straw bed platforms were absolutely swarming with fleas. It was a very miserable time. 'How can we possibly survive this?' Corrie wailed.

Betsie turned the question into a prayer. 'Lord, help us to see.'

Their one glimmer of light and hope in that terrible place was centred around the illicit prayer and Bible reading time that they had in their room with other room mates. Great strengthening and encouragement came from these daily meetings.

One Bible passage in particular captivated their interest:

"Be joyful always, pray continually, give thanks in all circumstances, for this is God's will for you in Christ Jesus."

There was much they found they could be thankful for: they were thankful that they were together, they were thankful that they could have a Bible with them; and they thanked God for the crowds of people with them that could hear His Word through their circumstances. And then Betsie thanked God for the fleas. 'How can I be thankful for fleas?' Corrie wondered indignantly.

This story gives a brilliant illustration of how a negative situation can be given the Opposite Reaction Treatment. They didn't want the fleas. They didn't want to be in that cruel, foul, smelly, oppressive place. None of it was nice, and very little of it could raise genuine thankful feelings in them. Especially not fleas!

But Betsie had taken the verse to heart, "give thanks in all circumstances", and she put a positive opposite reaction in place, so that it could repel the very natural inclination to complain and mope.

The conclusion of this story was amazing.

One evening, Corrie arrived back from a wood-gathering foray, and found Betsie waiting for her, so that they could join the food line together. Betsie's eyes were twinkling. Corrie asked Betsie what she was looking so pleased about. Betsie responded by recounting what she had overheard that day. 'You know, we've never understood why we had so much freedom in the big room', she said. 'Well I've found out!'

During that afternoon, there had been some confusion about sock sizes in the knitting group. The prisoners had asked the supervisor to come and settle it, but she wouldn't come in. She would not step through the door.
'Do you know why?' Betsie could not keep the triumph out of her voice. 'Because of the fleas. That's what she said. "That place is crawling with fleas!"'

Yes, there was blessing even in the fleas, Corrie discovered. Because of the fleas, the ladies in their overcrowded, foul-smelling bunk room were spared from harassment, and had a measure of freedom that they otherwise might not have had. Their Bible study was unhindered. All because their supervisors refused to enter a room that was so overrun with fleas.

"Giving thanks in all circumstances" is only possible when we, like Betsie, employ a positive opposite reaction to the negative situation or feelings that we might have.

No, it's not easy. There are many things that we might very legitimately have no gratitude for.
How can we say thank you for a marriage breakdown, the loss of a loved one, or a debilitating accident, for instance? Some things are not thankful experiences!

But could we learn, like Betsie, to find positive aspects around our negative experiences to be thankful for? This is where a positive opposite reaction helps us out.

Betsie Ten Boom never did get to be released from the concentration camp. She died of illness within the camp. But her determination to cultivate gratitude, no matter what, did give her a release of sorts. It gave her release from the prison of her mind, allowing her to experience a joy in the moment that would not otherwise have been possible.

Two men in prison looked out from the bars of the window. One saw mud, the other saw stars. Thankfulness helps us see the stars. Like the Apostle Paul, we can learn to say:

"… I have learned to be content whatever the circumstances. I know what it is to be in need, and I know what it is to have plenty. I have learned the secret of being content in any and every situation, whether well fed or hungry, whether living in plenty or in want. I can do all this through him who gives me strength" (Philippians 4:11-13).

What a beautiful example of how cultivating thankfulness can help us towards living with contentment in our lives.

Pest protection

Our chapter began with butterfly houses. These enclosures are designed to be a protective haven for the little creatures that live within them. They are meant to protect them from the pests and predators that might be out to harm or kill them. Without protection, caterpillars are susceptible to any nasty pest that might happen along.

Our own journey toward transformation is fraught with pests and challenges that inhibit our growth. One of the ways that we can give ourselves protection from some of these pests is to practise thankfulness. This beautiful attitude can be a real lifesaver, and a game-changer.

Let us take up the challenge to find gratitude in every aspect of our daily lives.

In a nutshell:

- Thankfulness is a practice that helps protect us from the nasty pests of ingratitude, grumbling, dissatisfaction, envy, inferiority …

- Thankfulness honours God, helps change our attitude, and helps to enhance our overall physical and mental health.

- We can help shift our focus by finding a positive opposite reaction.

- The lens through which we view the world is what becomes our reality.

Prayer time:

'Thank you, Lord, for providing us with the blessing of thankfulness. Thank you that this can work as a protective factor in our lives, against the things that would drag us down. Please help us to learn to practise thankfulness. Please help our thankful attitude to grow. With deep gratitude for your love, Amen.'

Chapter 6

Growing gratitude

'Be thankful in all things', is what He has said.
It now depends on what my thoughts are fed!
For sure, it's not easy, but victory is near,
With joy a reward for a heart full of cheer!

"Rejoice always, pray continually, give thanks in all circumstances; for this is God's will for you in Christ Jesus" (1 Thessalonians 5:16-18).

"And whatever you do, whether in word or deed, do it all in the name of the Lord Jesus, giving thanks to God the Father through him" (Colossians 3:17).

PRACTISING thankfulness is a helpful aid towards gaining balance and perspective. It is a beautiful life-enhancing practice to engage in. It is also a practice that helps offset negativity. Whether negativity may cause us to feel dissatisfied with our features, form, personality, or life in general, creating a gratitude habit can be a helpful antidote.

Developing gratitude will take some training. However, there are disciplines that we can practice to help grow an attitude of gratitude. We will consider some of these in this chapter.

Just as a butterfly house provides a protective enclosure to the little creatures within, practising gratitude can help us build a protective covering for our hearts from the pests of negativity.

A butterfly house needs to have a foundation, walls and a roof for it to work as a protective enclosure. Gratitude can operate in a similar way. To protect our heart from pests, let's lay some good gratitude foundations. This will be followed by some 'walls' to help keep unwanted attitudes out. Finally, we will top it all off with a good 'roof'!

Foundations

FOR gratitude really to flourish, it needs a good foundation.

Scripture

Our best foundation for establishing a thankful heart, is through God's Word. It is our anchor point, giving us reasons and encouragement to be thankful. Filling our minds with helpful verses, comforting verses, challenging verses and reassuring verses will help us gain a sense of peace that God is in control, even when we feel out of control. Meditating and absorbing these verses will help us towards a joyful spirit.

We need to find verses that speak peace and assurance to us, and keep reminding ourselves of them.

I recall one Bible camp, where the speaker gave all of us Bible verses to memorise. Each day he gave us a new one.

The verses he gave us have stayed with me to this day. They are my anchor verses, my go-to places of assurance.

On occasion I have even put music to them, so that I could sing the verses as continual reminders.

One of those beautiful verses comes from Philippians 4:6,7:

> "Do not be anxious about anything, but in every situation, by prayer and petition, with thanksgiving, present your requests to God. And the peace of God, which transcends all understanding will guard your hearts and your minds in Christ Jesus."

What an amazing foundation this verse gives. This is what it tells us:

- Don't be anxious.

- Instead, pray.

- Present requests with thankfulness.

- God's peace will guard our hearts and minds.

What an amazing blessing to have peace guarding our hearts, rather than anxiety running fruitless circles round it!

There is so much blessing and reassurance that comes from God's Word. It is there for us to read and memorise. It is a sure and solid foundation for encouraging growth in thankfulness.

Pray

Alongside reading and memorising, comes prayer. As the verses from Philippians tell us, "present your requests to God, by prayer, petition and thanksgiving".

One of the ways we can build thankfulness through prayer is to ask at the beginning of each day:

- What can I be thankful for today?

- What can I learn to appreciate about myself?

- What can I learn to appreciate about the people around me?

- Please help me to see beauty in all that's around me.

- Please help me to express thanks to you for all these blessings every day.

Then we must listen and be aware of impressions that come to mind. Each new day we are presented the opportunity to see it through gratitude inspired eyes.

At the conclusion of the day, a prayer of thanks helps cement the thankful thoughts in place. All that has happened in the day can be subjected to the treatment of thankfulness, and offered to God as a sweet smelling sacrifice of thanks and praise.

Rest

It might be stating the obvious, but it is very hard to think thankful thoughts, and be sweetness and light when we are overtired, wound up and stressed out.

We have already talked about the need to care for our bodies through providing adequate rest, but let's remind ourselves of its benefits.

I know that it's not always easy to get sufficient rest. There are times in our lives where sleep is not quite what we would like it to be, for one reason or another. Sometimes this is unavoidable, such as the season of life with young children. This will need to be weathered through as best we can.

At other times, lack of rest is due to the frenetic pace of life that we allow ourselves to have. This can include the need to hurry. We can feel that we need to push as much as we can into a day, which escalates the rush problem. Rushing around affects our gratitude and love. It is difficult to experience and engage in gratitude moments when we are rushing around and much too busy.

To offset this problem, and to give balance, God introduced a day of rest for His people. The Sabbath was specifically given to allow people to have the rest that they needed. We don't tend to operate by the same laws as the Israelites, but the principle is still a good one for us to practice.

At one point, I decided that a Sabbath rest day would be a good thing to implement. On Friday evenings, at 6 pm, I would stop work for the day, and we would begin the evening with a candlelit dinner. The day that followed, Saturday, I would prioritise time to the practice of what I called the three 'R's: Rest, Recreation and Relationships.

I found that taking a rest day was a very worthwhile discipline to follow. Even now, although our practice of observing a specific rest day has slipped, I still like to think that the three R's can be given some priority one day in the week.

A rested body and mind are a good place to start growing the gratitude attitude.

So, the foundations we need to build our gratitude on are Scripture, prayer and rest.

Walls

WITH good foundations in place, we can now think of some other disciplines and strategies to help gratitude to grow. These are practices that help put a protective wall around our hearts to ward off negative attitudes, and to enhance our lives with beauty. There are four walls: thankfulness diary, praise, celebration and perspective.

Thankful diary

Writing down what we are thankful for is a good way to begin training our minds towards thinking thankful thoughts. The written word has the benefit of being visual, and is a reminder for us in days to come of what we had previously been thankful for.

A while ago, I suggested to my younger daughter that she should start a thankful diary. Every evening she would write down three things that she was thankful for from that day. At one stage she asked me if I was also keeping a thankful diary. She was rather indignant when I admitted I wasn't. So to make amends, and to practise what I was preaching, I also started keeping a thankful diary. It is incredible how the simple task of writing down thankful thoughts promotes a greater sense of joy. Thinking of my 'best things' for each day has most definitely grown a greater sense of overall appreciation for all sorts of things. At one point, when I felt I was taking my husband a bit too much for granted, I started writing down what I appreciated about him for each day also.

He trumped me at this game, however. One year, he produced a diary in which he had filled in every day of the previous year with things that he was thankful for about me. Every day he had written in something different that he appreciated. It was a most beautiful gift to receive; but he was the one who benefited the most from it. Why? Because all those thankful thoughts that he had written down over that year had cemented and ignited a thank-filled and appreciative attitude towards me, which helped his love to grow stronger.

Such is the beauty of expressions of thankfulness, and the good that it does for us.

Praise

> "Give praise to the LORD, proclaim his name; make known among the nations what he has done. Sing to him, sing praise to him; tell of all his wonderful acts" (Psalm 105:1,2).

Praise is a verbal expression of thanks. It is a great discipline to implement in our lives. It helps counteract the low periods in our lives, and focuses our mind on the positive.

Praise is part of living a God-centred life. The Psalms are full of praise, and instructions to praise. God appreciates us praising Him.

Praise to God, when used in song, combines both music and words which are wonderful tools to elevate our minds and give us a sense of well-being. Words that are expressed in praise encourage the mind to think of positive things. It also promotes the awareness of having a powerful God who is worthy of that praise.

It is interesting to note that we don't have to 'feel' in the mood for praise to engage in it. If we were to wait until we felt like it, we would very rarely actually do it! But praising, even when we don't feel like it, can have the effect of changing our feelings to be more aligned with the praise itself.

I experienced this very powerfully one day. I was standing in the kitchen, looking out of the window at all the work that needed doing in our yard, and was feeling quite dejected about the seemingly endless amount of tasks that needed to be done. Recognising that I was on a very negative thought path, I started to sing some praise songs. I didn't feel like singing. I felt more like having a pity party. But an amazing thing happened. After a little while of singing, I discovered that I actually wanted to sing. The more I wanted to sing, the more I enjoyed it; and the more I enjoyed it, the more positive I felt. By the end of that time of praise I was really tuned into it. The negative feelings had receded, and I felt a greater sense of peace.

Praise does not have to be just song. Words of praise and thanks can be expressed in any way. Praising out loud is a good practice however, as it reinforces the words in our minds.

Celebration

"A cheerful heart is a good medicine, but a crushed spirit dries up the bones" (Proverbs 17:22).

Engaging in moments of celebration is one of the ways that we encourage a cheerful mindset, which in turn creates gratitude-filled hearts.

Celebration moments are numerous. They could be inspired by a beautiful sunset, dew drops on the roses, jumping in puddles, laughter, the song of a bird ... These are moments where we turn aside and stop to appreciate a moment of wonder. We pause our busyness long enough to hear, observe and engage.

Maybe celebration moments will come in the form of strenuous exercise, a hobby, craft or gardening ...
Maybe they will come with the elation gained by achievement, especially in an area that had previously been challenging.
Celebration moments can come with holidays, outings and trying new activities. Healthy fun activities give us moments to celebrate.

Robert and I have been having date nights together for many years. Sometimes it can become quite routine; still enjoyable, but in need of a revamp. Having heard the suggestion of having each date night based around a different letter of the alphabet, we launched into an A-Z date night extravaganza. That really gave our date night a fresh look and awakened our creative juices.

For example, our letter 'B' date night consisted of a 'B'-themed dinner: beef and beetroot burgers, broccoli, beans, bean sprouts, followed by banana and blueberry smoothies. Robert says he's never had a burger with green beans on before! Then we read a book and enjoyed a bath together.

Alphabet dates were moments of healthy fun that gave us a sense of celebration, and a cheerful spirit.

Celebration moments also come with the realisation that we have been able to forget ourselves long enough to invest time, energy and love into someone else.

Our son Jeremy tells us that he loves to start random games at Youth Gatherings. When he sees a group of young people just sitting around in a circle, he goes up to them, and, with great energy, goes round the group tapping heads and chanting: 'Duck, duck, duck ... goose.' He gains a great deal of pleasure and amusement to get a game of duck, duck, goose happening with a group of teenagers. Once he has infected the group with enthusiasm to participate, he leaves and watches them carry it on.

Celebration lies in enjoying the moment, embracing the journey, and living with eyes open to the beauty and possibilities that are all around us.

Get perspective

Another protective, and enhancing practice to help us grow gratitude is perspective.

As we look back over the years, we can see how God has worked in our lives, and has brought us through many a tough moment. This encourages us to keep going with a confidence that is gained by seeing how God has worked in our lives in the past.

Alongside that, we can take inspiration from the people around us who, despite some great challenges in their lives, keep pressing on. They live life as fully as they are able, given their situation. Many continue to reach out to others, giving of themselves, despite their own struggles.

Perspective helps to confine fears that might otherwise overwhelm us.

Roof

OUR protective haven of thankfulness needs to be completed with a roof. A roof gives a protective covering, and keeps the 'rain' out. A roof can only sit on top of existing walls and foundations, so taking care of our 'foundation' and our four 'walls' is important.

Joy

Joy is a beautiful fruit of the spirit. It is an attribute that is built on the 'walls' of thankfulness. Without thankfulness coming first, we cannot have joy.

Joy is something that fills our hearts with a peace and tranquillity that is outside of our circumstances. Whether life is a bed of roses, or whether it is being stuck in a stinking prison, joy lifts our hearts and spirits above our situation.

Rejoice

"Rejoice in the Lord always. I will say it again: Rejoice!" (Philippians 4:4).

For Paul and Silas, these words were more than just a concept. They lived this reality in the most awful of circumstances.

Paul and Silas had been thrown into prison in Philippi because they had healed a poor slave girl. They had been severely flogged, then thrown into a dark, damp inner cell, and their feet fastened in the stocks. Bleeding backs, excruciating pain, tired, no doubt frustrated at their treatment, Paul and Silas did something wonderful. They began to sing praises to God.

It was midnight when Paul and Silas were praying and singing hymns to God. The other prisoners were listening in amazement.

What gave them motivation or reason to sing with such joy in these circumstances?

They focused on thankfulness. They were thankful that they had been counted worthy to suffer shame for Christ. That perspective produced overwhelming joy within them, which in turn burst out of them in the form of praise. They sang praise with genuine joy that they could suffer for Christ, despite the pain.

What an amazing example of rejoicing in the face of suffering.

The power of joy at work in our lives gives us freedom from our circumstances, and enables us to have a measure of peace.

What a beautiful protective covering joy gives to us.

Joy-spreaders

We could all do with spending some time with joy-spreaders. Joy-spreaders are the people that we just love to be around. They raise our spirits, inspire laughter, have positive encouragement, initiate spiritual conversations and help point us in the right direction. They motivate us, and encourage us to grow. They inspire us to be the best person we can be.

I love spending time with my cousin. She challenges and encourages me. I enjoy our spiritual conversations. My heart burns within me through the sharing of thoughts from God's Word together. We part company with me feeling lifted up and motivated.

She inspires joy in me.

As well as spending time with joy-spreaders, we should aim to become a joy-spreader. Be the one who invests into others with encouragement and love.

We can aspire to pass on joy and encouragement through our words and our presence.

There are always ways that we can invest into other people, and create moments of joy for them.

Let us make someone else's day today by words and actions that inspire. Let us create moments that promote joy and happiness.

Joy and rejoicing are the roof that sits on top of our four walls and foundation. These create a beautiful completion to our thankfulness structure.

Protecting our heart

Thankfulness is a wonderful discipline that helps protect our heart from the nasty pests like grumbling, dissatisfaction, envy, inferiority or even superiority.

We have a good foundation through God's Word, from which we can build habits and actions that will help us tune our minds towards thinking thank-filled thoughts. As we develop this mindset, we will grow a greater disposition towards joy; that beautiful fruit of God's Spirit.

The practice of gratitude is something that will help enhance our sense of value. As we look at ourselves as a precious work of God's creation, we will be able find many things to thank Him for. As we look at others as a precious work of God's creation, we will be able to find things in them to thank God for.

What a beautiful protective, and life enhancing, haven thankfulness can be.

Praise be to God for His wonderful gifts; for all He has done, and is doing. Thanks be to God for all His many blessings!

In a nutshell:

- God's Word, prayer, and rest provide the foundation for building thankfulness into our lives.

- Writing thankful thoughts, expressing praise, engaging in moments of celebration and finding perspective all provide good structure for developing a habit of gratitude.

- Joy is the beautiful fruit of God's Spirit that gives us peace and tranquillity in the midst of whatever situation we might be in. Joy cannot be a factor in our lives without first practising thankfulness.

Prayer time:

"I will sing to the LORD all my life; I will sing praise to my God as long as I live. May my meditation be pleasing to him, as I rejoice in the LORD" (Psalm 104:33,34).

Chapter 7

A good work

'Trust me in this', He said, 'for I have a great plan,
A life of purpose for you, as for all of man.
Place your confidence now in what I can do
For you, and with you, it surely is true!'

"'For I know the plans I have for you,' declares the Lord, 'plans to prosper you and not to harm you, plans to give you hope and a future'" (Jeremiah 29:11).

"Being confident of this, that he who began a good work in you will carry it on to completion until the day of Christ Jesus" (Philippians 1:6).

THE caterpillars on the swan plant were encountering another problem. What had started with a large amount of small caterpillars, had now turned into a large amount of bigger caterpillars; with big appetites! The plant had been eaten to almost nothing. It was a stalk in the ground, with very little edible life left on it. Assuming caterpillars are even capable of making decisions, now was the time to make some big ones. For them to continue to grow and change they needed more food.

Here is where the situation became interesting. The caterpillars all had to disperse to find food. One caterpillar ended up in the vegetable garden, on a lettuce leaf. Not much scope for food there! Another one had obviously 'decided' that looking for more food was too hard, and it had spun itself a cocoon – even though it really was not quite ready for that stage of transformation.

Still others had made the arduous journey across the pavement to find another uneaten swan plant, which now became home. This new food supply was just what they needed to continue their growth and change in the right way. Although their journey towards transformation had encountered a challenge, they had not let it get the better of them. There was more growth and change ahead, and they were focused on what needed to be done.

The dilemma the caterpillars faced reminds me a little of what life can look like for us.

We have a starting point for transformation. This is the healthy diet of value that is rooted in God's love. No matter what others think of us, or even what we think of ourselves, God's Word assures us that we are loved and wanted. Value has been bestowed by this love.

We have considered the protective and enhancing practice of thankfulness. Practising thankfulness helps protect us from the nasty pests of negativity that are out to rob us of life.

But we can't remain here. It is still only the beginning of our transformation journey. We need to grow. God wants us to grow the value He has invested into us. Our transformation journey is all about change and growth.

One of the ways that we grow value is through investment. But it's going to take work!

Jesus told a parable in Matthew 25 about a man going on a journey who entrusted his property to his servants to look after. To the first servant he gave five talents of money, to another two talents, and a third servant was given one talent. The distribution of the money was given according to each servant's ability (see verse 15).

The servant who had been given five talents got to work and gained five more talents, giving him a total of ten. Similarly, the servant with two talents also doubled his, giving him a total of four. The one talent servant was a bit fearful, and went and hid his talent in a hole he had dug in the ground.

On his return, the master called his servants together to get his money back and to receive a report on what they had been doing while he was away. The five and two talent servants were commended for their wise use of the money. The one talent servant was given a scathing rebuke. He was called "lazy and wicked" for burying what had been entrusted to him.

His problem was not that he didn't have as much as the other two, but that he didn't grow what he had been given.

We have all been given 'talents'. We have all been gifted with personality, ability, time, energy and potential. According to the parable of the talents, that which was entrusted to each of the servants came with an expectation that it was meant to grow. It was meant to become more. It was meant to be invested. This is going to take work, but according to the parable, it is achievable!

It's worth considering what we might learn from the habits of the one-talent man, and the two-plus talent men.

Deadly habits of a bury-your-talent person

There are some lessons we can learn from the one talent man in the parable. The quantity of what he had been given was not relevant, it was the attitude towards his mission that was the key point of Jesus' story. Here are some unfortunate habits and attitudes associated with burying our talent:

- Believing that we don't amount to much because we are not as gifted as the five or two talent person.
- Not valuing the talent that has been entrusted to us.
- Letting fear rule our lives.
- Engaging in negative self-talk.
- Focusing exclusively on the 'hard' side of the Master's character.
- Burying and ignoring the talent we've been given.
- Being lazy.
- Having no action plan.
- Allowing problems to negate any action.
- Not being prepared to take growth risks.
- Choosing not to invest.
- Lacking trust in God.

I have seen some of these scenarios at work in my life. Too frequently I have passed up opportunities because of fear. I'm not skilled enough. I fear failure. I fear rejection. I fear being thought of as incompetent. So I stay confined to a narrow world, so that I don't mess up. When fear has the upper hand, it paralyses action, halts momentum and inhibits my growth.

Allowing fear to have the upper hand in our lives is a deadly habit.

A while ago, I heard this inspirational thought: 'We miss 100% of the shots we never take.' These words were written on the base of a neglected and unused basketball hoop. How true this is. Fear can hold us back from taking the shot. True, it might keep us from the embarrassment of missing the hoop, or dropping the ball, but we will never know if we might succeed in our shot if we don't try. Not only that, but mistakes are an integral part of learning.

Failure, or not achieving the desired result that we want, does not need to be the end of the story. Instead, it can become a platform to learn from and a process to grow from. Perhaps something will need modifying about our venture. Perhaps we will decide it was a wrong move after all. Perhaps we will know it is a right move, but it needs some perseverance fully to succeed at it. Perhaps it will be first shot success: 'ball goes through hoop'. None of these scenarios will be obvious without trying first! Success is not usually about perfect first time results. It's more about trying, perhaps failing, and trying again.

Growing our talents also involves wisdom. Wisdom is needed to show the where, when, what and how to use our talents. Our loving God is just waiting for our call to ask for this wisdom. It's free for the asking!

Talents grow from trial, error and use.

Peter opened the way for this sort of growth within himself with his water walking experience. Peter and the other disciples were out in a boat at night, in a storm. The wind and waves were battering the boat, and even these hardened men of the sea were afraid. They were still a considerable distance from shore as the day was beginning to dawn. It was at that moment, as light was just appearing, and shadows were taking on defined shapes, that Jesus came out to meet them, walking on the water. This absolutely terrified the disciples; they had never experienced someone walking on water before, and they were convinced that it couldn't be a real person. At their cries of fear, Jesus gave them a message of reassurance: "Take courage! It is I. Don't be afraid" (Matthew 14:27).

Peter had a daring thought, but he needed some reassurance about the wisdom of his adventurous idea:

"Lord, if it's you", Peter said, "tell me to come to you on the water" (verse 28).

"Come" was the reply.

With Jesus' invitation to come, Peter left the safety of the boat and negotiated the wild stormy waters. The other disciples watched in awed fascination. Fear, disinclination and disbelief would all have been legitimate feelings for these men at this moment. Perhaps they were also feeling disdainful of Peter's seeming impulsive and rash decision to get out of the boat. As they watched, however, they would have seen something amazing. For a few awe-inspiring moments, Peter actually walked on water. It was only when he took his eyes off Jesus, and focused on the wind and the waves, that he began to sink. Jesus reached out his hand and caught him, gently rebuking his doubt and fear. As Jesus and Peter climbed into the boat with the other disciples, the wind was subdued, and all was calm on the water.

This whole incident concluded with everyone in the boat worshipping Jesus. They acknowledged him as truly being the Son of God!

Fear did not inhibit Peter's resolve to come to Jesus on the water. The problem of water not being solid enough to walk on – let alone this particular lot of water being turbulent – did not deter Peter. The invitation to "come", gave him enough courage for that moment to get out of the boat. He grasped the moment, and he took the risk. In later life, Peter would have had this life-changing experience to draw comfort from. He loved and trusted Jesus enough to get out of the boat and go towards him. He had a few mind-blowing moments of water-walking by faith. He was saved from drowning by Jesus when his faith suffered a setback. He witnessed how the saving miracle of Jesus inspired worship in all the disciples. All these things he would not have experienced first-hand if he had remained in the boat. Success for Peter came in trying. He didn't have a perfect first time result to his mission, but he would have learned some very valuable lessons from his attempt. As time went on, Peter's confidence in Jesus, his ability to follow in Jesus' footsteps with miracles and wonders, and his appointment as 'rock' of the early ecclesia all came on the back of his earlier tentative steps of faith. His growth came by learning from his failures. There was no fearful talent burying for Peter!

Effective habits of a two-plus talent person

What might we learn from the two-talent man in Jesus' parable? What are some of the attitudes, habits and beliefs that he would have been practising? In what way can we grow like the double-your-talent person?

- He appreciated having two talents, and got on with using them. He didn't compare himself to the five-talent person, or gripe at only being given two.

- He tried hard. He worked hard. He gave things a go.

- He worked with what he had been given, and he doubled it.

- He didn't allow setbacks to disable his achievements. He practised, expanded and persevered.

- He valued, and counted as precious the talents with which he had been entrusted.

- He respected and trusted the Master sufficiently to desire to work hard for him.

Respecting what God has entrusted us with, is a key element of what we can learn from our two-talent man. When we put comparison aside, and get on with the task of growing that which we've been given, we will start to see two talents becoming four. Or five talents becoming ten. One talent can also become two if we allow it to grow. It is not that life is somehow much easier for those with two or five talents; it is just that they have grown the tenacity and perseverance to keep trying. Obstacles and challenges become a platform for growth.

Moving on from Peter's early tentative steps of faith out on the water, Jesus later commissioned Peter with the task of "feed my lambs", and "take care of my sheep". Talents were being distributed, and these were the tasks that Peter was entrusted with. Peter rose to the challenge. After Jesus' ascension, at the time of Pentecost, Peter stood in front of a large crowd of people and fed them the word of truth, life and hope. He warned and pleaded with them. That day, about 3,000 people responded to the message Peter gave, and lives were saved. Talents were given, talents were multiplied.

Peter's example shows us what talent growth is all about.

God confidence

"Being confident of this, that he who began a good work in you will carry it on to completion until the day of Christ Jesus" (Philippians 1:6).

Knowing that God's work in us will be completed is the basis of our confidence. It is a God-based confidence. This confidence is the foundation for growing our talents. We are who we are because of who God is. We are wonderfully made because we are created in His likeness. We are called because God chose to call us. We are strong because of God's strength.

God has begun a good work in us and He will bring it to completion. He has entrusted us with talents, faculties and abilities. There are good works to do, tasks to accomplish, daily lives of purpose to engage in. There are people to love and care for. There is good news of the gospel to share.

We have been made on purpose, for a life of purpose. We are no mistake. We are not a random puzzle. We are not an apologetic piece of humanity; an 'oops' on the landscape. We are not even a self-made person. We have been made on purpose, for a life of purpose.

God has given us life, endowed us with bodies and personalities. He has gifted us with talents, interests, and abilities. He has prepared 'good works' for us to do. He is willing to take the person we are right now, with all our flaws, and work with us to develop us into something even more. He will carry on this work in us to completion, if we cooperate and let Him. Our task is to grasp the talents and value we've been entrusted with, and put it all to work.

When value is invested it grows.

All my life, my self-confidence has been low. My confidence in myself and in my abilities has been little. But I am learning God-confidence. I know that He can take that raw material (some of which I cringe at), and turn it into a work of art, for His glory. His strength is made perfect in my weakness, and my weakness can only be made perfect in His strength.

Whether you tend towards timidity like I do, or whether you are a naturally bold and confident person, God-confidence is the surest foundation. This sort of confidence is one that expresses that God has begun a good work in us. It accepts the gifts and faculties that He's given. It takes opportunities. It acknowledges God's strength, and His ability, and puts it all to work. Talents are doubled, trust and confidence in God grows, and God is glorified.

Back with the caterpillars on the swan plant, I recall a most perplexing scenario. There have been a number of times that I have seen a caterpillar on its journey across the ground in search of more food, and I have decided to help it out. I have picked up the little creature, and taken it to another uneaten swan plant. I felt like I had saved it a lot of time and energy by short-cutting its journey. But here is where it became perplexing: the caterpillar would sometimes choose not to stay on the plant. For whatever reason, this plant was not to its taste, and it would later be seen wandering aimlessly across the pavement again. 'Silly caterpillar', I would think, 'I am trying to give you what you need, and you are refusing to take advantage of it! Why?'

I don't have an answer as to why a caterpillar might turn its nose up at what seems to be a perfectly good food supply, and wander off, leaving the food behind.

But it leaves some food for thought. Do we sometimes also pass up the opportunities for growth that might have been given to us? Do we sometimes say 'no thanks' to the value investment and growth God would like us to have?

It's worth thinking about.

Life is purposeful. At least it should be! With good works prepared in advance for us to do, let us go on to explore what purpose and tasks lie in front of each of us.

Talents and good works have been distributed. Value has been received. Value can now be invested to make it grow.

In a nutshell:

- God has begun a good work in us, and will bring it to completion.

- We have been made on purpose, for a life of purpose.

- We've been entrusted with 'talent'. Whether it is one, two or five is irrelevant. The most important thing is what we do with what we've been entrusted with.

- We can be confident of God's purpose for us and with us.

- The value we have received from God's love should be invested to achieve growth.

Prayer time:

'Dear Lord, please help us to see the "good work" that you have begun in us. Please help us to rest in the confidence that you have a purpose for us. And please may we utilise those talents that you have entrusted to us. Please help us to see that our lives are more than just living out an existence of self-centred interest until we die, and that it means more than just marking time until Jesus returns. Help us to see your purpose for us and to grow it. May we lean on you, for you are all-powerful and all-knowing. Amen.'

Chapter 8

A life of purpose

"For we are God's handiwork, created in Christ Jesus to do good works, which God has prepared in advance for us to do" (Ephesians 2:10).

I LOVE this verse from Ephesians. It is an anchor verse for me. It tells me that I am God's handiwork. I have been created by Him – and we know that He values what He has created and invested so much into! The word "handiwork" gives me the impression of a craftsman who is at work on what he is creating. He is moulding and forming his creation to help it become all that it can be.

This verse also tells me that I am created in Christ Jesus to do good works. When I dedicated my life to the Lord, I began a new life in Christ. This new life in Christ is meant to be a purposeful life of good works.

Furthermore, those good works have been prepared in advance by God for me to do. This is truly awe-inspiring!

But it does pose a question: What are the good works that God has prepared in advance for me – and you – to do?

The main purpose of "good works" is to enable us to live purpose-filled lives that will honour, serve and respect the One who made us. If we have been created in Christ Jesus, then we should be showing Christ Jesus to all around us with what we do. Showing Christ is our highest calling.

So the question, 'what are the good works that God has prepared for us', is a probing and an important one. "Good works" are to help us show and respond to God's love for us. "Good works" are one of the ways we show Christ to the world.

"Good works" are also one way in which we grow the value God has invested in us. We have opportunity to create further value for God's glory by what we do with our time, resources and energy.

There are some wonderful case studies in the Bible that give us practical insight on how the person in the story used their opportunities, time, energy and resources in a purpose-filled way. Their stories have been recorded in God's Word as a testimony to their good work, and as a source of inspiration to us.

One of those stories is about a slave girl. This young Jewish girl had been captured by a raiding band of Arameans. Her life of freedom, as a loved daughter of her family, came to an abrupt end with her capture. She became a slave to the wife of a man named Naaman.

Naaman had leprosy – a deadly disease.

The young girl knew that if Naaman would go and see the prophet in Israel, he could be healed. She didn't hold back. She did not allow bitterness, anger or self-pity to stop her from passing on the crucial information that she had. She passed the precious information on to her mistress, and urged her to tell Naaman to go and see the Prophet.

We can refresh our memory on how this story plays out by reading it in 2 Kings 5. Meanwhile, long story short, Naaman was not only physically healed, but got to have a life-changing encounter with the God of Israel.

What an amazing moment of purpose this young girl had. She took the opportunity she had been given and rose to the task. She created value by her words. Her good work created the opportunity for another person to be impacted by God. The simple thing she did was written down to inspire us to live in the same way.

Another lady who created value by one significant purposeful act, was the lady who came to anoint Jesus' head while he was dining in the home of Simon the Leper. Her story is recorded in Matthew 26.

This woman came with a jar of very expensive perfume. This perfume would have cost her a lot of money.

There was no doubt in this woman's mind as to what she intended to do with it. She arrived at Simon's home, and followed through with her intention, of showing Jesus honour and love, by pouring her perfume over his head.

Her actions earned her criticism by the disciples, and possibly many of the other guests. They reasoned that the perfume could have been sold for a high price, and the money given to the poor.

Jesus, however, received her gift with grateful acknowledgment.

> "The poor you will always have with you, but you will not always have me. When she poured this perfume on my body, she did it to prepare me for burial. Truly I tell you, wherever this gospel is preached throughout the world, what she has done will also be told, in memory of her" (verses 11-13).

What a privileged purpose this lady had! She got to anoint her Lord before his death and burial. It was more than just perfume that she poured; she poured out love. She was giving him what few others recognised that he needed, or were prepared to give.

What a beautiful moment of purpose this lady engaged in that day.

There are so many more stories we could draw upon. People who ministered to needs, spoke the right word in season, gave of their time and resources, and some who even forfeited their very lives for their purpose.

Each of them lived life purposefully. Frequently it was in everyday ways; at other times it was playing their part in significant one-off situations.

So we return to the original question. What are our "good works" that God has planned in advance for us to do? How can we create value with intentional living?

Before we consider some ideas of how we can live lives of purpose and good works, there is an important warning to consider.

The verses preceding Ephesians 2:10 say this:

"For it is by grace you have been saved, through faith – and this not from yourselves, it is the gift of God – not by works, so that no one can boast" (verses 8,9).

Here is a big 'caution' sign highlighted for us. It is easy for our works to become what we think defines us, or gives us value. Sometimes we allow work to become the thing that gives us a sense of significance. This can become yet another detour in our attempt to measure value. While on the one hand we are expected to live purposeful and work-oriented lives, it is not the work in itself that gives us value. In fact this verse specifically tells us that works will not earn us value. We cannot earn 'brownie' points, as it were, by the works we do. Works done for that reason will take away from the salvation that is offered to us by grace.

So we tread a fine line. We live purpose-filled lives of good work, but it is not that which defines our value.

The way we create value through our work, is by how we respond to God's love with what we do. It is the way we give of ourselves to others. It is the way we impact the lives of other people that creates value for God's glory. And, yes, we can rightfully feel a sense of pleasure and fulfilment through giving of ourselves in this way, but we need to keep perspective in everything.

Our sense of significance is often tied up in the work that we do. It can be a crushing experience if something happens to the work we have relied on for our sense of identity.

Robert has experienced the feeling that goes with a loss of significance when he was no longer able to do all the "good works" he had previously been involved in due to burnout. He had been very busy working for the Lord in a number of different ways. His life was full to overflowing with service. He loved contributing in this way. But then burnout came, and along with that came the inability to be able to contribute in the way he had previously been doing. He experienced all the feelings that come from loss of purpose. That which had previously given him a sense of fulfilment and purpose had been taken away due to his poor health. What is more, many of the roles he had previously done in our ecclesia were now ably being filled by others.

This was a humbling experience for him.

There were two factors that kept him from falling into a state of dejection over his loss of purpose. The first one was that he kept reminding himself of the verse that says:

> "And we know that in all things God works for the good of those who love him, who have been called according to his purpose" (Romans 8:28).

The other factor was that he kept telling himself that since God was in control of everything, then it would be God who would provide new direction and purpose for him when the time was right.

Both of these perspectives were helpful in alleviating the pain that accompanied his loss of purpose and significance.

It is useful for us also to keep a similar perspective toward any work that we do. Knowing that God is in control will help keep us balanced in our attitude towards what we do.

With all that said, let's think of some of the ways we can create value through the "good works" we do; how we can live purpose-filled lives, and how we might know what the good work is that has been prepared in advance for us to do.

Asking and listening

"If any of you lacks wisdom, you should ask God, who gives generously to all without finding fault, and it will be given to you. But when you ask, you must believe and not doubt" (James 1:5,6).

The Bible contains many instructions about the generic good works that we should be engaged in. These are all specifically from God, so it is a really good place to start when we are looking for good works to do! Our ultimate purpose is to love God, and to show Christ to the world in all that we do and say.

As far as individual good works go, it is a bit more of an undefined area. However, there are some ways in which we can prepare ourselves to be more open to the God-sent opportunities that lie in front of us.

The simplest way to start to understand what good works God wants us to do is to ask. Pray. We can ask God if there is anything specific that He would like us to engage in. We can ask Him how we should be using our energy that day and what our priorities should be.

One lady I know begins her day with this prayer: 'Lord, these (listed) are the activities that I think I will be engaging in today; however, if you have different plans for my day, please help me to see them, and I will be open to following through with your plans instead.'

There is a lot of room for improvement for me in this practice. Frequently I make my own to-do list for each day, without first praying for God's guidance and blessing over it. Being a task-oriented person, I find myself getting frustrated if my to-do list gets derailed by other pressing needs. When someone or something crops up in my day that I did not expect, I can find myself getting annoyed at the interruption of my plans. This identifies a problem for me: I do not always ask for God's direction for my day, and even if I do, I am not always listening or responding to what He might give me.

I suspect I miss many opportunities of God-given good work because I am too focused on the work I have appointed for myself!

There are occasions, however, that I have turned aside from my own plans to take up opportunities that come my way. Whenever I have done this I have always been very glad about it afterwards.

One of those occasions occurred for me on an early morning walk one day. I was intending to get through my walk, and then get home to progress through a busy schedule. As I came round a corner, I happened to see an acquaintance walking the opposite way on the other side of the road. I was tempted to wave and smile a hello, and keep walking. I was very focused on my busy schedule for that day.

However, I did cross the street, and we engaged in a few moments of conversation. It turned out that this lady had recently lost a baby granddaughter. She was on her way that morning to go and visit the grave of this infant. I had the opportunity to reach out a hand of sympathy, and say a few words of support.

All this I would have missed if I had kept on walking, intent on carrying on with my own plans. Afterwards, I felt very uplifted that I had paused my own plans for that brief moment to invest into someone else.

So, in answer to the question of what good works we should do, we find that, first, Scripture will help us find answers to what our good work should look like in the big picture.

And secondly, asking God in prayer about our specific everyday purpose is another thing we can do. But we need to listen to the answers that come through the opportunities that present themselves. This involves follow-through – which is an area I certainly need to work on!

Good works have been planned in advance for us to do. What might that look like for you?

Faculties and talents

"Having gifts (faculties, talents, qualities) that differ according to the grace given us, let us use them: [He whose gift is] prophecy, [let him prophesy] according to the proportion of his faith; [He whose gift is] practical service, let him give himself to serving; he who teaches to his teaching; He who exhorts (encourages), to his exhortation; he who contributes, let him do it in simplicity *and* liberality; he who gives aid *and* superintends, with zeal *and* singleness of mind; he who does acts of mercy, with genuine cheerfulness *and* joyful eagerness" (Romans 12:6-8, AMPC).

Another aspect to good works, service, and purposeful living is linked to our personality type.

God has gifted us all with different personalities, abilities and interests.

The verses above, from Romans 12, place our abilities, broadly, into three categories: speaking, organising and serving. Most of us would resonate with one more than another. Some people thrive on public speaking, others are much more at home serving behind the scenes. Others are happiest organising everyone else. Each have an important part to play, and are needed for service in the community.

Being gifted with a speaking ability can be utilised in many creative ways. I know one sister who has used her speaking ability to run Bible Seminars for other women. She does an amazing job of it, and has impacted the lives of many other women over the years with her knowledge of the gospel. I have heard of others who have run Bible reading groups in their homes. And many have dedicated time to Sunday School teaching.

But using our ability to speak is not limited to a group or a formal setting. Speaking personal words of encouragement to others and talking to people on a one-on-one basis are constructive ways we can use our gift of words.

A talent to serve also has a lot of scope. Hospitality, practical service within the ecclesia, meals for others, visiting the sick. The opportunities are endless!

The people who have a talent for organisation have their special part to play also. Those of us who would much prefer to be given direction, greatly appreciate the organisational skills of those who can direct!

These characteristics and abilities are placed within us by God. Our job is to find what we resonate with, what service in that area might look like for us, to extend ourselves in it, and to bless others through it.

Every day purpose

"Likewise, teach the older women to be reverent in the way they live, not to be slanderers or addicted to much wine, but to teach what is good. Then they can urge the younger women to love their husbands and children, to be self-controlled and pure, to be busy at home, to be kind, and to be subject to their husbands, so that no one will malign the word of God" (Titus 2:3-5).

Every day we are given the opportunity of engaging in intentional living. Every day we have good work to do in living purposefully. God has given us the precious gift of time. What do we do with it?

Everyday life can look a bit mundane, and we can find ourselves feeling that it lacks the exciting areas of good work that we might rather be involved in. However, giving ourselves fully to the responsibilities that have been placed in our lives does give glory to God.

The verses from Titus are all about living purposefully and fully in the everyday areas of our lives. To love our husband and children. To be busy at home. To keep the home operating in a God-based manner.

Let's think about a few of the areas of responsibility that might be in our lives.

- **Responsibility of a wife:** If we are married, then our responsibility to our husband is to love and respect him. Everyday we have opportunity to bless him with our service, love and support. We can aim to be the best wife we can be to our husband.

- **Responsibility of a mother:** If we are a mother, we have the precious responsibility to love and nurture our children. We have been given the awesome task of shaping and helping them to develop into responsible adults. We have the amazing privilege of introducing them to God. We have opportunity to pray for our children and grandchildren.

- **Responsibility of a daughter:** We are all daughters! If our parents are still alive, we have responsibility towards them. They are the special people in our lives who have helped us become who we are. We have opportunity to bless and love them. We honour them and God in doing this. In their times of need, we have the awesome privilege of caring for them.

- **_Responsibility of a sister or auntie:_** Many of us have siblings or close relatives that we can invest time and love into. We can be there to listen, encourage, support and care. We can become an adoptive auntie to somebody else's child. Everybody loves to be given some attention, and to be noticed. Let's especially look out for the lonely. There is a lot of scope for showing care and interest as a sister or auntie.

We can fill in a job description for every area of our lives that falls under our responsibility. This can include being an employee, an employer, a home-maker, a friend, a neighbour, a teacher, a mentor ...

The list could go on.

One couple that I know have some wonderful stories of how blessing their neighbours has led to establishing some lovely friendships. Their caring actions have created an amazing opportunity to witness to their faith. All without them having to do any formal preaching!

When a storm whipped through their area, and left the neighbourhood without power, this couple sprang into action. Even though they were new to the area, and didn't know some of their neighbours yet, they visited people, asking if anything was needed. Since they had a generator, they were able to loan it out to others to keep their refrigerators operating.

One neighbour made this comment: 'You are Christians, aren't you?! Most people don't act like this today.'

What a wonderful way to 'witness' to their neighbours by living an ordinary life of God-honouring good work.

All around us are countless opportunities we can purposefully take advantage of, to bless the precious people in our lives, both those we see regularly, and those who might live further away.

Even the mundane task of housework is a lovely gift for our families, creating an oasis of peace at home for everyone to enjoy.

Whatever we do, let us do it as if we are doing it for God. We honour Him when we serve, bless and love others to the best of our ability! We are a witness to others about Him in our actions and attitudes.

That brings us to another point that is worth mentioning. How can we live purposeful lives of contribution when we have physical or mental impairments? Life can be much more restricted in times of old age, or when we have some sort of disability.

Even in age or disability we still have some valuable things to offer. Maybe all we can do at that stage of life is to pray for others. Maybe we can pick up the phone and make a call to encourage someone. Maybe we can send a card. Just giving someone a smile can make a big difference. All of these things continue to create value through blessing. There is always something that we can contribute.

My mother decided, quite some time ago, that she would live each day as if it were her last. She resolved to do good in whatever way she could for anyone who came her way. When she discovered she had an aneurysm in her aorta that could burst at any time, she started to add 'I love you' to the conclusion of any conversation she had with family members. She wanted every interaction to count. It was her chance to express love. Life is too short to live with the regrets of lost opportunities. For her, sleepless moments during the night became a chance to pray. She would pray every day for each of her children, her twenty grandchildren, and twenty-one (plus) great-grandchildren. What a gift she was giving to each of us, what an amazing blessing.

She is now over ninety, and her physical abilities are limited; but what she still continues to contribute to her family, and her ecclesial family, is priceless.

Everyday living might not seem that glamorous at times. But if we are living purposefully and intentionally every day, we can create value in our lives with a beautiful rich tapestry of good works. Along the way we might encounter times of special purpose moments, just like the young slave girl, and the woman who anointed Jesus. But generally our purpose every day is to fill in our 'time sheet' with service, blessing and doing the best we can right where we are.

May we live purposeful lives each and every day, giving God glory by the way we spend the time He has given us. May we seek His wisdom, and rely on His strength, so that the good work He has planned in advance for us to do, may be operational in our lives.

In the next chapter we will discuss further thoughts on creating value, this time through confident living. Our talents and abilities are given to us to grow, and to use to bless others. When we develop a confidence that is based on God, and what He can do with and through us, our ability to grow and use what we have has a great foundation. The stories of Ezra and Nehemiah give us some good case studies to draw inspiration from.

Meanwhile, let us take this gift of today and create blessing and value with the time we have been given.

In a nutshell:

- We are God's handiwork, created in Christ Jesus to do good works, which have been planned in advance for us to do.

- The Bible contains wisdom on what good works look like. For more specific answers on what good work might look like for us, we can ask God, listen, and follow through on the opportunities that come along.

- Our personality types are all different. The type of work we might be drawn to will differ according to our faculties and talents.

- Everyday purpose lies in front of all of us. We can bless those around us by fully engaging in purposeful service and love.

Prayer time:

"And this is my prayer: that your love may abound more and more in knowledge and depth of insight, so that you may be able to discern what is best and may be pure and blameless for the day of Christ, filled with the fruit of righteousness that comes through Jesus Christ – to the glory and praise of God" (Philippians 1:9-11).

Chapter 9

Living with confidence

"Now to him who is able to do immeasurably more than all we ask or imagine, according to his power that is at work within us, to him be glory in the church and in Christ Jesus throughout all generations, for ever and ever! Amen" (Ephesians 3:20,21).

"I can do all things through him who strengthens me" (Philippians 4:13, ESV).

THERE is nothing quite like knowing that a Divine Being has created us, and given us life on this earth. There is something special in knowing that the Divine Being is our heavenly Father, who loves us. We know that He loves and values us, because He paid an enormous price to show us! It cost Him the pain and death of His dearly loved Son, our Lord Jesus.

In addition to the assurance of being loved and wanted, God has given us purpose. All those who have said 'yes' to His offer to be a part of His family in Christ, have been given 'good works to do'. We have been created on purpose, for a life of purpose.

The "good works" are part of how we create value in our lives, for God's glory, and to His honour. Doing good works to God's glory gives a sense of significance that is beyond ourselves. It is more than just finding meaning in what we do. It is belonging and being connected to something – Someone – bigger and higher than ourselves.

With God at the centre of our lives, we have purpose. Real and fulfilling purpose!

Knowing God's love and plan for us gives us confidence that our lives have meaning and purpose.

"Being confident of this, that he who began a good work in you will carry it on to completion until the day of Christ Jesus" (Philippians 1:6).

In the previous chapter, we began to look at some of the ways we can create value through purposeful living. In this chapter we continue to explore purposeful living through a growing confidence in what God can do with and through us.

The action-packed lives of Ezra and Nehemiah are great illustrations of living a purposeful life based on confidence in God. The concepts we will look at in this chapter were highlighted in their lives. Their response to God's calling, their preparation and their actions are all inspirational in regards to them living a confident life based on God.

Seventy years of captivity, as proclaimed by God, had come to an end for the Israelites. The time was right for them to return to their land and rebuild. Ezra and Nehemiah were key players in this mission. The gracious hand of God was upon these men. God appointed them a special task to aid the return of the exiles and help with the rebuilding of Jerusalem.

God's purpose was about to impact their lives dramatically ...

Prayer

Ezra and Nehemiah both began their mission with prayer. From the time they felt called to action, they turned to God in prayer, seeking His direction and blessing. They asked, listened and followed through.

Ezra was a well educated and devoted Levite, descended from the high priest's line. King Artaxerxes had allowed Ezra to accompany a group of exiles back to Jerusalem, along with a great quantity of silver and gold. The journey back was going to be dangerous. Ezra began his mission on the best possible footing. He proclaimed a fast, and petitioned God in prayer. Ezra was going nowhere, and doing nothing, without first seeking God's blessing and care.

Nehemiah's story also begins with prayer and fasting. He was saddened by the state of affairs in Jerusalem, and dearly wanted to go back to help rebuild it.

God answered Nehemiah's prayer by allowing the king's heart to be responsive to Nehemiah's request. So Nehemiah was given leave to return to Jerusalem to help his people rebuild the city. Nehemiah returned, ready and enabled for action.

Living a life of purpose should always be encompassed by prayer. Whether we are a homemaker, or one who is destined to live an action packed life on the edge, purposeful living begins with prayer.

Ezra and Nehemiah knew the importance of starting their mission with prayer, enlisting God's direction and aid. This is equally important for us.

I recall a time of asking God for some life purpose and direction. I was feeling purposeless, particularly in regards to my contribution within the ecclesia, and I wanted to know in what way I could address that.

During the week following that prayer, I felt drawn to the Parable of the Lost Sheep. A sense of direction started to crystallise for me through those verses. At much the same time, Robert had also been praying a similar prayer for purpose and direction. As we later talked of our separate experiences, we were amazed to learn that we had both felt drawn to the same thing. This was further confirmed in our minds by the number of people and opportunities that came our way during the following months. It was like God was encouraging us to reach out to people who were 'outside of the box'. Here was opportunity to engage in purpose through the doors that opened to us. The restless feeling of lack of purpose faded into the background as a confidence in God's direction began.

Confident, purposeful living begins with prayer.

Contribution and service

Another step towards confidence in creating value is to believe we have something to contribute to the world around us. God has made us wonderfully well, and has given us value. We belong, and we all have something to give – things we are good at, or educated about. These skills and knowledge need to be shared or used to inspire others.

Once we recognise that we have something of use to give or share, our confidence to use it grows. Our sense of worth and value will also grow with the realisation that we do have something to contribute in life.

We have seen this realisation blossom in our youngest daughter. As a toddler, she would often repel people's attention by shouting 'Shy' at them. She outgrew this tendency as she got older, but still remained shy and lacking in confidence.

When she learned how to crochet, it all began to change. Having an artistic personality, she enjoyed learning a new craft. Crochet gave her a means to create things to give away. It also gave her a teaching skill to share with her peers at school.

As our daughter realised that she had something to contribute, her desire grew to learn other new things.

After crochet it became cake decorating.

Realising she had something to contribute and become good at, has helped her confidence grow immensely.

My mother-in-law has used her skills to help people of different languages learn English. Her patient tuition has helped many a person learn and cement their knowledge of the language. She has also been instrumental in doing cooking tutorials in her home to help others learn new recipes. She has used her skills to bless others.

Ezra began creating value through contribution at an early age when he became skilled in understanding God's law. Long hours of study filled him with knowledge and zeal for God's way. This was evident even to the king, who blessed Ezra with these words:

> "And you, Ezra, in accordance with the wisdom of your God, which you possess, appoint magistrates and judges to administer justice to all the people of Trans-Euphrates – all who know the laws of your God. And you are to teach any who do not know them" (Ezra 7:25).

Ezra took this to heart, and determined to use his skills to serve and instruct.

> "Because the hand of the LORD my God was on me, I took courage and gathered leaders from Israel to go up with me" (verse 28).

Ezra's courage was ignited through God's equipping, and through his own diligent attention to what he was able to contribute.

In a similar way, our confidence to contribute grows when we realise we have something to offer. We can do this by learning and growing skills that we are drawn to and blessing others by sharing them.

Use failure as a step to learning

There was a problem among the remnant people in Jerusalem. Many had married foreign wives and were living contrary to God's law.

Ezra and Nehemiah recognised this as a big problem. It was because of these errors, and others like them, that Israel had been displaced from their land in the first place.

They pleaded with the people to learn from their history so that they would not be like their ancestors who disobeyed God. They asked them to turn from their wicked ways and commit themselves anew to God's ways.

The failure of their predecessors was to become a learning tool.

Failure because of disobedience is never a recommended way to learn; there are far more effective means! But it highlights the concept that, whatever the nature of failure is for us, it can be a platform to learn from. Failure can become a step on the way to learning – if we let it.

Confucius said: 'Our greatest glory is not in never failing, but in rising every time we fall.'

Thomas Edison succeeded in inventing the light bulb. It involved 1,000 unsuccessful attempts. When asked, 'How did it feel to fail 1,000 times?' Edison replied, 'I didn't fail 1,000 times, the light bulb was an invention of 1,000 steps.'

Henry Ford, the founder of the Ford Motor Company, said these words: 'Failure provides the opportunity to begin again, more intelligently.' In his attempts to make a car, Henry had failed and gone broke five times, before he succeeded.

These people didn't see failure as failure – or a full stop. They saw it as a step on the way to learning.

I recall a talk where the speaker told us of his workplace motto regarding failure: 'Fail quick, fail often and fail cheap.' This practice got successful results the quickest. It was recognised that failure, in some measure, was a part of every process, so 'fail quick, fail often and fail cheap'! This is a practice that can also help us grow. It will help us be prepared to see any failure as a learning opportunity. Value can be added through the growth attached to this learning.

Sometimes, as in the case of Israel, it will mean we have to change our direction completely. Other times, as in the case of Henry Ford and Thomas Edison, it will mean persevering until we succeed.

Let us be willing to use failure as a step towards learning.

Take achievable steps of progress

If we try to do too much too soon, or bite off more than we can chew, it can result in a nosedive. This can seriously undermine any confidence in being able to achieve our desired result. Taking small and achievable steps can help avoid this scenario.

Seeing success in the little steps taken, builds confidence and encourages continued progress.

We saw this in action with one of our daughters when she was developing water confidence. She loved being in the water, but always wanted to cling tightly to a parent. Robert would encourage her to jump to him from the side of the pool, by standing close to the edge and holding out his arms. As she tried it, and discovered it was both achievable and fun, Robert would move further back. Eventually, our daughter would reach the water before his arms grabbed her. With these gradual encouraging steps of learning, our daughter became quite water confident.

It was the small incremental steps of progress that enabled the outcome. If Robert had stood too far back in the first instance, our daughter would have been too fearful to try. By gradually increasing the distance, the desired result was achieved slowly but surely.

Nehemiah used this strategy with the people in the rebuilding of the wall. The wall was in a really bad state. In its entirety, the task would have looked daunting and insurmountable. The Jews' enemies certainly tried to convince them that it was an impossible task!

But Nehemiah spurred the people on to believing that it was possible to achieve, by getting each family or person to work on a small bit of wall that was designated to them. For many families, that meant working on the wall directly outside their house.

With each person doing their little bit, the work was done slowly but surely. They put their hearts and backs into the work, and God gave them victory.

Because the repairs were manageable for each family, they believed it was possible.

Confidence grows with taking these small, achievable steps of progress. Next time we are faced with a task that seems too big and overwhelming, let us take a leaf from Nehemiah's book, and break the task down into small, achievable steps.

Work with the resources that we have

The work on the wall was under threat. The Jews' enemies were plotting and scheming to stir up trouble for the workers.

After praying about this issue, Nehemiah then organised guards to be posted on duty day and night. It was a tough time for the people. It was difficult for the work to continue under the handicaps they were encountering. The strength and morale of the people were giving out.

Here is what Nehemiah did:

"Therefore I stationed some of the people behind the lowest points of the wall at the exposed places, posting them by families, with their swords, spears and bows. After I looked things over, I stood up and said to the nobles, the officials and the rest of the people, 'Don't be afraid of them. Remember the Lord, who is great and awesome, and fight for your families, your sons and your daughters, your wives and your homes'" (Nehemiah 4:13,14).

Nehemiah calmly assessed the situation. He organised people, and distributed the limited resources they had. He encouraged the people to trust in God and not be afraid. He utilised the resources that were on hand.

When we are faced with a problem, how do we react? Do we go into panic mode? Or do we, like Nehemiah, face the problem, and calmly assess what resources are at our disposal to resolve the issue at hand?

Our God-based confidence grows when we can learn to analyse our options and resources. Like Nehemiah, we can then take our resources, shore up our trust in God and face our situation. Our success, no matter how small, will improve our confidence for when we meet life's next problem!

People interaction

We had a very shy young man come to our house for dinner one evening. His confidence to interact with people was minimal. Never once did he make eye contact with us, and conversation was stilted. Eventually, he thawed out enough to participate and even make conversation; but we still never got to make eye contact.

It reminded me how much eye contact and posture speak of confidence. Clear eye contact expresses confidence in what we have to offer. It shows the person we are talking to that we are interested in them and in what they have to say.

Nehemiah had a lot of people problems to deal with. Not a problem with eye contact, or posture, I suspect! He had to face challenges to his leadership and authority. Not only did he face those issues directly, he did not allow the threats that were coming his way to intimidate him. He faced each person squarely as he dealt with their contention.

Nehemiah's difficulties were faced head on. Allegations were refuted and the work completed – despite the setbacks. Nehemiah's greatest strength in facing opposition from people came through God.

Nehemiah's enemies were trying scare tactics:

"They were all trying to frighten us, thinking, 'Their hands will get too weak for the work, and it will not be completed'..."

This is how Nehemiah dealt with the problem:

"But I prayed, 'Now strengthen my hands'" (Nehemiah 6:9).

This was the result:

"So the wall was completed on the twenty-fifth of Elul, in fifty-two days. When all our enemies heard about this, all the surrounding nations were afraid and lost their self-confidence, because they realised that this work had been done with the help of our God" (verses 15,16).

What a contrast! The enemies of Israel based their confidence in self. Their own strength failed them when they saw that God had given the Jews victory in the building work. Nehemiah's confidence was based on God's help and strength. His basis of confidence was the winning one. It overrode the opposition.

When God is for us, who can be against us? This was certainly Nehemiah's belief!

Let us, like Nehemiah, place our confidence in God. Whether our contact with people is challenging, or whether it's a pleasant interlude, let us enlist God's help to have positive and confident interaction.

Believe!

God wants us to succeed in confidently living out our God-given purpose throughout our lives. He has crafted us, gifted us, and equipped us to live a life of purpose. God has bestowed value on us from our conception onwards. He has given us faculties and talents. He wants us to step up and use those talents responsibly.

Our confidence is based in God. We belong to Him, He made us, and His love has given us value.

Let us believe that we have purpose, that we are precious to God, and that He has begun a good work in us. As we set out to create value in the world around us, let us do it with a confidence that is based on God's guiding hand in our lives. Let us live full and purposeful lives for God's glory.

"The LORD makes firm the steps of the one who delights in him; though he may stumble, he will not fall, for the LORD upholds him with his hand" (Psalm 37:23,24).

God is there to help, to hold us up, and cheer us on. Let us give God thanks for the grace and potential He has given us, and begin to live that out confidently, knowing that He is with us. Let us take up the challenge to grow what has been entrusted to us. One talent can become two or more when we graciously accept what we have been given and put it to work.

As we come to the end of the chapter, we will just take another look in on the caterpillars on our swan plant. It's been a while since we visited.

There are now some really large healthy caterpillars on the plant. They have eaten their way towards readiness for some significant change. The next stage of their transformation is almost ready to begin. This is an exciting development to watch. It's also a good reminder for us that we still have further change and development ahead.

Follow me through to the next Section of the book where we will pick up the story again.

But before we go there, it's time to review what we have learned.

In a nutshell:

- Our life in Christ is designed to be purposeful. We have been made on purpose for a life of purpose.

- Creating value in the world around us is a part of how we live a purposeful life.

- Building confidence in what God can do with and through us will enable us to face our tasks in life most effectively.

Prayer time:

"Now to him who is able to do immeasurably more than all we ask or imagine, according to his power that is at work within us, to him be glory in the church and in Christ Jesus throughout all generations, for ever and ever! Amen" (Ephesians 3:20,21).

Chapter 10

Section One conclusion

WE are loved! We are precious to our loving God. He allowed His most dearly loved Son to suffer a most terrible death, so that we could see and understand the depths of His love. Our loving Lord Jesus submitted his body to this horrible death, so that we could have life – new and abundant life – through him.

This love is the source of our validation, our sense of purpose and our reason for life. Every other way that we attempt to find significance in life is false. Comparison, people validation, work achievement – these are all things that will give temporary fulfilment at best.

The best foundation for successful life and growth is found in resting firmly in God's love and purpose for us. This gives us a sense of security like nothing else can. We are wanted. We have purpose. We are not a mistake. We are not here just randomly.

Because we are loved, and have purpose, we have a responsibility to create further value in our lives by caring for our bodies, growing our talents, living lives of good work and filling our minds with gratitude. This gives honour to the One who made us for His glory.

We began this book with a tale of two butterflies. One had emerged from its chrysalis with deformed wings. The other emerged with strong, healthy, vibrant wings. Along with some others, they had begun life as small caterpillars living on a swan plant. We have watched them grow. They have encountered pests, and have negotiated the challenge of having to find another swan plant for food when their original one was eaten. The caterpillars have arrived at the point where they are ready for a significant life change.

The caterpillars have been creating a picture for us. The process of change that they have been going through is similar to some of the change processes we encounter. There is much we can learn from them.

Our feet are on the road towards transformation. Our faces are turned in that direction. May the potential that God has placed within each of us be unlocked and released as we continue on this transformational journey.

May we grow strong and healthy 'wings' that will help us become all that God intends for us to be.

I have paraphrased a God's eye view of us, taken from some of the Bible verses we have looked at so far:

'Daughter, you are my child, and I have made you fearfully and wonderfully well. In my own image are you made, and that which I created from the beginning I have made "very good". I have created you with purpose and have planned good works in advance for you to do. You can have great confidence in this, for I love you, and there is nothing that can separate you from my love – except yourself. I am able to do immeasurably more for and in you than you might even ask for, by my power, that is at work within you.

'I want you to know that I am God, all-powerful and all-knowing. And I want that knowledge to fill you with joy as you live out your life with thankful praise, yes, in all circumstances. Then you will be a great fruit-bearer in every good work that you do. It pleases me to see my child living out her purpose, growing in knowledge of me, strengthened by my great power through all spiritual wisdom and understanding.'[1]

As we continue on into Section Two, let us remember all the groundwork of love and value that we have established so far. It will be helpful for the next stage of our journey of change. We are about to dig deeper into spiritual transformation.

---

1   Psalm 139:13,14; Genesis 1:27,31; Philippians 1:6; Ephesians 2:10; Romans 8:38,39; Ephesians 3:20,21; Psalm 100; 1 Thessalonians 5:16-18; Colossians 1:10-12.

Section Two

Chapter 11

Increasing by decreasing

"Whoever humbles himself like this child is the greatest in the kingdom of heaven" (Matthew 18:4, ESV).

"Whoever exalts himself will be humbled, and whoever humbles himself will be exalted" (23:12, ESV).

'God loves us so much that He accepts us as we are ... But He loves us too much to leave us that way' (unknown).

IT was time. The largest caterpillars on the swan plant had grown to the optimum size for a caterpillar, and were now preparing to make their momentous change. One had crawled its way to a nearby leaf on the swan plant, and had curled itself into a hook shape. Over the next little while it would change significantly. Its body would darken. Then all of a sudden, it would seem, the caterpillar would no longer be discernible.

In its place would be a lovely light green chrysalis.

It would remain as a chrysalis for quite a while. It would not be greatly evident to the outward observer, but inside the chrysalis a lot of change would be going on. In about ten to fourteen days a butterfly would be ready to emerge.

It is time for some more change in us too. I am hoping that we can now identify some of the things that have not been serving us well in our lives. Comparison, reliance on validation from people, negative self-talk and seeking significance through work, among others. These are some of the things that are unsatisfactory in terms of establishing a healthy sense of value.

The pathway to healthy value comes from a foundation based on God's love for us. God's love bestows value. It gives us an assurance that we are loved, wanted, and that God has an ultimate purpose for us.

God expects us to grow and create value from what He has given to us. Whatever talent He has invested into us must be used and grown for His glory.

There is one more type of value to consider. This is a really big one, so the rest of the book will be devoted to its consideration!

This is value that increases by decreasing.

Increasing value

A value that increases by decreasing is one that goes completely against human nature. Our natural reaction is to be defensive against anything that we feel 'diminishes' us. The walls go up, the defending army arrives, and all the ammunition at our disposal gets deployed against whatever is threatening our sense of value. We want to protect our fragile self-esteem from anything that might pull us down.

But God is asking something very big of us. He is asking us to let go of ourselves, so that we can become something more. He is telling us that 'value' will increase for us when we decrease in all the ways that relate to our natural fleshly nature.

This is change of huge proportions. It's going to require us to unpack our bag of self, and to repack it with all the good foundation of value that we've considered so far. We will then need to tuck in that quivering lip, square up our shoulders, and bravely contemplate what God is asking of us.

And what exactly is He asking of us?

"Have this mind among yourselves, which is yours in Christ Jesus, who, though he was in the form of God, did not count equality with God a thing to be grasped, but emptied himself, by taking the form of a servant, being born in the likeness of men. And being found in human form, he humbled himself by becoming obedient to the point of death, even death on a cross. Therefore God has highly exalted him and bestowed on him the name above every name, so that at the name of Jesus every knee should bow, in heaven and on earth and under the earth, and every tongue confess that Jesus Christ is Lord, to the glory of God the Father" (Philippians 2:5-11, ESV).

Here it is. Here is what increasing by decreasing looks like. Our Lord Jesus humbled himself in all ways. He emptied himself, relinquishing any 'rights'. He is our example. We are asked to follow in his footsteps, and take on this same attitude. Spiritual transformation can only happen when we are prepared to let go of self.

The upside of this, is the increase in value that will happen through this process. Because our Lord Jesus humbled himself, he is now exalted to the Highest Place. He is given the Name above all names. He is exalted, and his Father is glorified through him.

We are offered 'promotion' in a similar way. "He who humbles himself [herself], will be exalted!" This may not be here and now, but it will come. Value will increase, but only if we are prepared to decrease.

What we are being asked to do is similar to the change that is required for a caterpillar. If the caterpillar had the power of doubt and reason, like we have, it might have paused in its transformation process to consider the wisdom of changing. It has known nothing different in its short life, other than being a caterpillar that gets larger and larger. Imagine if it were to say, 'I know what I am, and I am comfortable with being what

I am. I don't know what is to come, so I would prefer just to stay as I am! Besides, what if I lose my sense of identity? I don't think this change business is for me!' If the caterpillar were capable of this sort of reasoning, and able to prevent its natural transformation process occurring, it would remain just a large crawly grub. It would not become all it could become, because it was comfortable with what it was.

As we are well aware, God has not given caterpillars this sort of capability. Transformation is a naturally occurring process for them.

For us it is a choice. If we can believe God's Word, this choice will be the most life-changing experience we've ever encountered. What we can be is nothing like we are now.

But to increase, we must first decrease. Some significant changes lie ahead!

Why let go of self?

This is an important question. What is the motivating factor for us to want to let go of self? Letting go of self makes us feel so vulnerable. Apart from God telling us that it is something we should do, what is there that might encourage us to do it?

There is a verse in Philippians 2 that gives us some very compelling reasons we should be willing to let go of self. They precede the verses that tell what letting go looks like:

> "If you have any encouragement from being united with Christ, if any comfort from his love, if any common sharing in [fellowship of, NKJV] the Spirit, if any tenderness and compassion ..." (Philippians 2:1).

Encouragement from being united with Christ, the comfort from his love, and fellowship of the Spirit are three very compelling reasons to be grateful for our position in Christ. The gratitude that is inspired by encouragement, comfort, love and fellowship gives us great motivating reason to respond to God's instruction for us to let go of self. When these factors are coupled with tenderness and compassion, then we have some amazing reasons to enable willingness to let go of ourselves, and to allow God to change us inside out.

The love that God pours out on us, the love that tells us we are valued, should motivate us to respond with obedience to what He is asking of us.

It's never going to be an easy task; but taking time to remember the reasons we should be willing to let go, is a good starting point for obedient action.

In the chapters ahead, we will spend some time reminding ourselves of God's character. His character is shown to us very tangibly through God's dearly loved Son, our Lord Jesus. Remembering His character is important so that we can reinforce a sense of assurance that our Lord is a capable heart surgeon; which is what we need for our transformation! Besides, we are told that we need to be more like our Lord Jesus, so it is worth reminding ourselves of how he operates. Submission and grace are key factors in this.

Following that, we will consider three beautiful and important elements to transformation: Faith, Hope and Love.

But before we go there, we need to take an internal look at the state of our hearts. Our heart is the place where change begins.

So it's time to take a deep breath. Something more and better lies ahead, but there is the potentially painful removal of unwanted growth to happen first.

Value can increase, but only if we are prepared first to decrease.

In a nutshell:

- The last type of value we will consider is one that increases by decreasing.

- This is a vital step for the transformation process.

- Letting go of self is very difficult, and will be best helped along by remembering our foundation of value.

- Something better lies ahead, but first we must let go of self.

Prayer time:

'Dear Lord, please help us to have an attitude like our Lord Jesus. He is the ultimate example of someone who let go of self. Please help us through this process, because it is very hard to let go!
Amen.'

Chapter 12

Heart matters

'Don't be complacent', I now hear Him say,
'There's something within you that's not so okay!
Your form, it is true, is made wonderfully well,
But that heart that you've got needs some change, I can tell!'

"The heart is deceitful above all things and beyond cure. Who can understand it?" (Jeremiah 17:9).

"Who can say, 'I have kept my heart pure; I am clean and without sin?'" (Proverbs 20:9).

W E have a very high calling. We are called to be like Jesus. We are called to decrease in ourselves, so that God can increase us. This is where we, like the caterpillar, are prepared to let go of ourselves, and submit to a very vulnerable stage of change. For the caterpillar, the chrysalis is the enclosure that is responsible for some pretty impressive work.

So what is it that needs to change for us?

God is asking us to decrease in our natural fleshly nature. Our human nature is at variance with His nature. The Bible describes our heart as the driver for our natural inclinations. I don't quite understand why such a vital organ in our body gets the label of 'deceitful' pinned on it, but that is how it is described in the Bible.

"The heart is deceitful above all things and beyond cure ..."

Just like the chrysalis is the enclosure where change happens for a caterpillar, the heart is the place where change needs to happen for us.

I don't know about you, but I found that when I first decided to get baptised, I had no idea what my 'heart' was capable of, or even what repentance really looked like on a personal basis.

I was in my teens when I decided it was time to be baptised. I had some Bible instruction lessons with an older, wiser person of faith, to help cement my Bible knowledge, and to help me see the need for submitting my life to God.

During one of our discussions, the concept of repentance was brought up. I was challenged with this question: 'Do you realise the necessity of repenting of your sins, as you go through with this act of baptism?' Sure; I knew the theory, but I didn't really know what I was repenting of. I had lived a sheltered, unassuming life to that point. The 'little' sins were easily forgotten, and repentance was just a concept that didn't mean a huge amount to me.

Since that time, I have gradually become more aware of what my heart is capable of. God has slowly been working on me to help me see the darkness that I harbour inside. He is making me aware of the good that I omit to see or do. He is showing me, little by little, the need for repentance and how it is personal to me.

This stage of our transformation journey is not one that is designed to load us down with a lot of guilt. God is not making us aware of deceit and wrongdoing just to make us feel guilty;

or to have any greater sense of worthlessness than what we might already experience. He is wanting us to be aware of what is going on inside our 'heart' so that change can be made. Guilt is an emotion that doesn't serve us very well, especially if it pulls us down into a hopeless mess. Raising awareness of the deceit in our heart is for the purpose of necessary change, and to help us to draw closer to our Lord, as our source of strength. God desires for us to be set free from guilt and condemnation. That is why awareness of deceit is so necessary.

The Bible puts it this way:

"Godly sorrow brings repentance that leads to salvation and leaves no regret, but worldly sorrow brings death" (2 Corinthians 7:10).

The sorrow that God wants us to encounter with regards to our sinful state is a sorrow that leads us to repentance and life.

Heart deceit

What does a deceitful heart look like?

In Mark 7:21-23 our Lord Jesus outlined some of the deceitful things that the heart is capable of:

"For it is from within, out of a person's heart, that evil thoughts come – sexual immorality, theft, murder, adultery, greed, malice, deceit, lewdness, envy, slander, arrogance and folly. All these evils come from inside and defile a person."

In the book of Proverbs, we are told of seven things that the Lord hates:

"There are six things the Lord hates, seven that are detestable to him: haughty eyes, a lying tongue, hands that shed innocent blood, a heart that devises wicked schemes, feet that are quick to rush into evil, a false witness who pours out lies and a man who stirs up conflict in the community" (Proverbs 6:16-19).

These are lists of evil that God detests. They fall into two categories: sins of commission, that we go out and do, or sins of evil attitude.

I immediately think about David with regards to the sins of commission that were listed in the previous verses. David scored a bullseye on all of these: sexual immorality, murder, adultery, greed, deceit, shedding of innocent blood, and devising wicked schemes. In one fell swoop, his illicit relationship with Bathsheba caused a roll on effect resulting in a collision course with at least seven of the evils that God hates.

Maybe some of us can relate to aspects of this. Maybe some of us have slipped up, let our guard down, and now stand 'guilty as charged'. Maybe even reading this makes us cringe, knowing the way we have let God, and others, down.

If that is you, take courage and assurance; you are in company with a man who was called "a man after God's own heart". If we can show the same repentant spirit as David, we will be on the road that leads us to forgiveness, grace and healing.

The other type of deceit in our heart is what I call 'evil attitude' sins. These are things like evil thoughts, greed, malice, deceit, envy, arrogance, haughty eyes ... Maybe some of us could admit to some of these. Or maybe we wouldn't. The problem with an evil attitude is that it deceives even ourselves, and we can be oblivious to it in our lives. A bit like having a plank in our own eye, but only able to see the speck of dust in our neighbour's eye!

This type of deceit in our heart is a particularly tricky problem because of how easy it is to ignore, justify or be unaware of.

It's so hard to be repentant of something that we are either unaware of, or refuse to acknowledge.

The group of people who generally modelled this evil attitude well, were the Pharisees and teachers of the law in

Jesus' day. It's easy for us to spot this at work in their lives from looking in from the outside!

Jesus had a very descriptive word for these people. He called them hypocrites – a word that describes a play actor. A hypocrite is someone who lives life to make a good impression; but their actions are inconsistent with their words.

Jesus quotes from Isaiah with these descriptions:

"Isaiah was right when he prophesied about you hypocrites; as it is written: 'These people honour me with their lips, but their hearts are far from me. They worship me in vain; their teachings are merely human rules'" (Mark 7:6,7).

"For this people's heart has become calloused; they hardly hear with their ears, and they have closed their eyes. Otherwise they might see with their eyes, hear with their ears, understand with their hearts and turn, and I would heal them" (Matthew 13:15).

In short, these people looked like one thing on the outside, but were something else on the inside; they honoured with their lips, while their hearts were far from God's heart.

"Woe to you, teachers of the law and Pharisees, you hypocrites! You are like whitewashed tombs, which look beautiful on the outside but on the inside are full of the bones of the dead and everything unclean. In the same way, on the outside you appear to people as righteous but on the inside you are full of hypocrisy and wickedness" (23:27,28).

These people led lives that were also colourfully described by Jesus as "being full of the bones of the dead". They had hearts that harboured deceit, greed, malice, envy and arrogance. These can often be covered up on the outside, while on the inside they are alive and well. They are attitudes that are not necessarily apparent to anyone else, but are obvious to God.

While the sins of commission can become evident to anyone who might be looking on, the attitude sins can be very successfully hidden, even from our own selves!

The tragic result of letting these attitudes go unchecked is that the heart becomes hard.

Let's take a moment to check whether we might harbour a similar deceitful attitude:

- Every time we nurture envious thoughts about other people – coveting their popularity, lifestyle, success, spirituality or strength of character – we join the ranks of the Pharisees who envied Jesus in these ways.

- Every time we make judgements on someone else, think or say snide comments that pull another person down, we are like the Jewish leaders who accused Jesus of doing miracles through Beelzebub.

- Whenever we talk about someone behind their back, whispering with others – bringing up all the baggage we can on a person – we walk alongside the leaders of the day, who stirred up an evil report amongst themselves about Jesus.

- Whenever we say one thing, but act in a different way, we are also being hypocrites.

- When we honour God with our lips, but our lives don't reflect His character, we too worship in vain.

- Every time we try to appear better, more spiritual, more noble than we really are, we join the company of those who were described as whitewashed tombs.

Ouch! I don't know about you, but I found that a very uncomfortable exercise!

Trying to look better than what we are is called Impression Management. We want people to see only the good side of us.

We can become very good at hiding the not-so-nice stuff. Like the Pharisees and leaders of the day, we can become addicted to the drug of having people think highly of us. This means that there is an awful lot of hiding that goes on; we hide things from other people, and even from ourselves. Like the teachers of the law, when we practise Impression Management, we become either blind to our failings or good at justifying ourselves. None of us want to have the deceit in our heart discovered!

It's natural to want to hide the parts of ourselves that are not so pleasant. We are afraid that if people see us warts and all, they won't like us very much.

Interestingly, I have found that the people I often respect the most are those who have been able to be up front about their shortcomings. Rather than me thinking less of them for their weakness, I find myself respecting their courage, and wishing that I had the same sort of courage!

The Lord Jesus exposed the inconsistencies of the Jewish leaders, and their show-acting lives, in the hope that they would be able to see it and change.

Unfortunately, they didn't like being told they were wrong, and that they needed correction. All the weapons at their disposal came out, and the war was on against Jesus who was threatening their sense of value.

The most frightening aspect about a Pharisee response is the danger of becoming hard-hearted. Hard hearts are unmouldable, unteachable, and ultimately unchangeable. Hard hearts are blind to truth, and justify wrong attitudes and perspectives.

It becomes disturbing when we look further at the hard-hearted responses that the Jewish leaders had toward Jesus. As Jesus exposed their greed, loveless attitudes, inconsistent teachings and pride, their anger and hatred against him intensified. Instead of seeing a Messiah, whose words and actions were faultlessly consistent, they saw a threat to their leadership. Instead of recognising a Master Physician who wanted to heal them, they saw someone who did his miracles through the 'power of Beelzebub'.

Ultimately, their hard-hearted attitude led to them committing murder. It led to them justifying their actions by accusing Jesus of blasphemy. They chose to believe that it was better that Jesus be killed than to have the people 'led astray' by him.

It is no wonder that God abhors a deceitful heart! When a deceitful heart is left unchecked, it goes into the death throes of hard-heartedness from which there is no going back.

To save us from developing a hard heart, we need to submit to a heart health check, and we need to be able to admit to the darkness that's within us. We need to turn, and repent, and place our hands in the hand of the One who wants to give us some life-saving heart surgery.

The sad news is that we all have a natural tendency toward having a deceitful heart. Big heart problems, or small heart problems, we all have them!

Whether our problems with a deceitful heart have led to us succumbing to the sins of commission, or whether we tend toward the evil attitude sins, we are all in this together.

Maybe we are already miserably aware of the weakness within us, or the way in which we have fallen in a particular area. Maybe we feel we are unlovable with our inner ugliness.

Maybe we are unaware of what our heart is capable of. Maybe we have closed ourselves off to correction, so that we can protect our own sense of value.

Whatever description is true for us, now is the time for us to dig deep into our foundation of value, to remind ourselves that we are loved and wanted. Then slowly, maybe painfully, we will need to get to the point where we can let down the bars and walls that guard our hearts, so that the Lord can help us with the changes that need to be made. He wants us to succeed. Remember that He loves us so much that He accepts us as we are; but He loves us too much to leave us that way.

Our hearts are the enclosure where bad work happens. It's also the enclosure where good work can happen.

Out of all this work, we want to be like a butterfly that has developed wings that will work. That is why we want to choose to accept correction, allow change, and to turn to the Lord and be healed.

Since the time of Adam, the only man who has been capable of training, taming and overcoming his deceitful heart has been our Lord Jesus. He is now, not only our ultimate example of exemplary living, but is Highly Qualified to help us with our weaknesses. In his perfection of character, Jesus did not become judgemental, pious, or completely unsympathetic. Instead, it strengthened his ability to understand us in all our struggles.

He truly is God's most wonderful gift to all of us who battle with deceitful hearts!

Now would be a good time to pause in our heart analysis to remind ourselves how beautifully trustworthy, patient and loving our Lord is. If we are going to partner with him for change, it's good to be reminded how he operates.

We will do that in the next chapter.

Meanwhile, let us keep remembering that the pathway of increasing value happens through the decreasing of ourselves. It begins in the heart. Our thoughts, attitudes and perspectives prompt our actions. This is why a heart inspection, and a heart health check are so important.

What goes on in the heart really does matter!

In a nutshell:

- The heart is the place that is described as being "deceitfully wicked".

- To become more like our Lord Jesus, we need some change in our hearts.

- Deceitful hearts cause us to stumble. They result in the sins of commission and evil attitude sins.

- It is when we try to hide or deny that we have a deceitful heart, that it has the potential to cause the most damage.

- If our deceitful heart is not stopped in its tracks, it will lead to hard heart issues.

- What goes on in the heart really matters!

Prayer time:

Let us pray that God may awaken an openness to examine the motives and actions that our heart inspires. May He awaken a willingness within us, to bring to light that which is hidden.

Chapter 13

The trustworthy Lord

'Do you mean a heart transplant?' I hear my voice squeak,
'That's major business, I'm afraid I'm too weak!
Will it hurt, are you gentle? There's so much to ask ...
I'm sorry to doubt, but can I trust you with this task?'

"Let us draw near to God with a sincere heart and with the full assurance that faith brings, having our hearts sprinkled to cleanse us from a guilty conscience and having our bodies washed with pure water. Let us hold unswervingly to the hope we profess, for he who promised is faithful" (Hebrews 10:22,23).

"And so we know and rely on the love God has for us. God is love. Whoever lives in love lives in God, and God in them. This is how love is made complete among us so that we will have confidence on the day of judgment: in this world we are like Jesus. There is no fear in love. But perfect love drives out fear, because fear has to do with punishment. The one who fears is not made perfect in love. We love because he first loved us" (1 John 4:16-19).

"And I pray that you, being rooted and established in love, may have power, together with all the Lord's holy people,

to grasp how wide and long and high and deep is the love of Christ, and to know this love that surpasses knowledge – that you may be filled to the measure of all the fullness of God" (Ephesians 3:17-19).

OUR heart is the place where transformation has to begin; just like the chrysalis is the place where change happens to the caterpillar. The caterpillar can't become a butterfly without first logging time inside the chrysalis.

There is a vulnerable process that goes on inside a chrysalis in order to create a butterfly. It is a process that is not for the faint-hearted!

The work that needs to go on in our own hearts is not for the faint-hearted either. It would be really helpful to know that the One who is overseeing the operation is truly trustworthy!

Heart surgery

My mother has had two major heart surgeries. They were both because of an aneurysm in her aorta. The first surgery was an emergency one, done at midnight. She had little time to think about the implications of such major surgery, whether it was the right thing to do, or how trustworthy the surgeon might be. The aneurysm was on the point of bursting and there was no time for such questions. If her life was to be saved, she needed urgent surgery. By God's grace, the surgeon certainly did work skilfully that night, and the aneurysm was repaired.

With the second heart surgery, she had more time to think about it. This aneurysm was not quite so much on the point of bursting, but it did still need repair so that it wouldn't get any worse.

Through consultation, the surgical team decided they could repair this aneurysm without needing to do the same open heart surgery as last time. But it wasn't going to be altogether straightforward. They would attempt to put a stent in, but it would be a rather complicated stent, as it was a complicated-looking aneurysm. This time, there was plenty of opportunity for question, doubt, and fear of the unknown.

When it comes to our own spiritual heart surgery, it is only natural that there will be questions and fears. The diagnosis has been made: the heart is deceitful, and needs some urgent work if our life is to be saved. How well do we trust our surgeon? Are we prepared to let Him do all the poking and prodding, scraping and cleaning that needs doing? Are we prepared to trust Him with our fears, hurts, insecurities, hidden sins and general self-centredness? Are we prepared to submit to His ways and methods? It will be very invasive surgery!

Before my mother's second surgery, she met the surgeon. He introduced himself, explained what was going on, and proposed the best solution to the problem. He looked and sounded knowledgeable. He seemed trustworthy. It would have been a different matter if he had begun the appointment by telling my mother that he was actually trained as a butcher; but not to worry, the jobs were very similar. I could well imagine that, under those circumstances, my mother would have had some very grave misgivings about the wisdom of going ahead with surgery undertaken by a man trained as a butcher! Fortunately, it was nothing like that; my mother's surgeon had all the right letters after his name, showing that he had been trained in the right way and was the right person for that job.

We too need some heart surgery. We know that God wants us to be transformed in our minds and hearts; having our heart of flesh replaced with the heart of the Spirit, and to have minds that are willing to tune in to His voice. We can't do this alone. We need our heavenly heart surgeon to assist us with this. As this is such major surgery, it's worthwhile thinking about the character of our surgeon, to remind ourselves of how trustworthy He really is.

God knew how important it is to us to be assured of how trustworthy and caring He is. He arranged a very tangible, touchable, approachable, understandable way for that to happen. He sent us His dearly loved and altogether loving Son, so that we could look at the characteristics of His Son and understand a bit more of the heart of the Father. Our Lord Jesus came to show us his Father.

Hebrews 1:1-3 tells us:

"In the past God spoke to our ancestors through the prophets at many times and in various ways, but in these last days he has spoken to us by his Son, whom he appointed heir of all things, and through whom he made the universe. The Son is the radiance of God's glory and the exact representation of his being, sustaining all things by his powerful word."

So let us get to know our Lord Jesus a little more.

Our Lord knows us

The story of Jesus' interaction with the Samaritan woman at the well gives us some insight into his depth of knowledge of a person. It was remarkable in the first place that he engaged her in conversation at all. Even she was surprised. He was a Jew, and she a Samaritan. Jews and Samaritans keep their distance from each other; they really don't get along! But Jesus was undeterred by this drawback. He knows who will respond to him, regardless of race. He knows what's inside a person's heart.

As the conversation progressed, Jesus told the woman to go and call her husband, and then come back to hear more. She told him that she had no husband. Jesus responded,

"You are right when you say you have no husband. The fact is, you have had five husbands, and the man you now have is not your husband. What you have said is quite true" (John 4:17,18).

The woman was surprised. Not only did this stranger know her background and current status, but in the knowing of it, he still chose to make conversation with her! In her eyes, Jesus should have had at least three things against her: she was a Samaritan, she was a woman, and she had a very shady background. Surely no self-respecting person should be seen hanging around her, especially a Jew. This one must be a unique and unusual person!

In her excitement, she hurried back into the town to tell everyone there about Jesus.

"Come, see a man who told me everything I ever did. Could this be the Messiah?" (verse 29).

This story gives us great comfort. How wonderful it is to know that our Lord knows us, and in the knowing, still chooses to spend time with us. He hasn't been turned off by the knowledge of our dubious background, race or gender. He has still reached out the hand of friendship, acceptance and hope – if we choose to accept it.

What a privilege it is to be known and accepted by Jesus!

Our Lord is approachable and touchable

This next encounter was with the woman suffering from bleeding. All women know how it feels to have a regular monthly period. But this poor woman had ongoing bleeding. To make it worse, under the law, bleeding meant a person was unclean. They were impure for at least seven days, and anyone who touched them was also made unclean. Their clothes and their bed were unclean. They were untouchable. To touch someone with an issue of bleeding was to make yourself unclean also. This lady had been unclean and untouchable for twelve years.

She knew that Jesus had the reputation of being a great healer. Rather than expose him, and everyone else, to the knowledge of her uncleanness, she thought she would just quietly slip in and touch the hem of his garment. He need not know anything about it.

But Jesus did know. He felt that power had gone out of him. He knew that someone had touched him. And he knew that when they had touched his garment they had been healed. Her touch wasn't going to be left as a secret, he sought her out in that crowd. Who had touched him? Trembling, she came forward.

Now she was exposed. She had to confess to what she had done and why she had done it. Her uncleanness was broadcast to everyone. And with that telling would also come the knowledge that Jesus was now tainted by association with her uncleanness.

"Daughter, your faith has healed you. Go in peace" (Luke 8:48).

How wonderful it is to know that our Lord is so approachable and touchable. How amazing it is that, despite our weakness and impurity, he is still willing to acknowledge us and allow us to reach out to him. How incredible it is that he is willing to associate with us, even though we also are unclean because of sin.

Our Lord is compassionate

Jesus was in a town called Nain with his disciples and a large crowd was following him. As he approached the town gate, a dead person was being carried out. He was the only son of his mother, and she was a widow.

Scenes like this must have been common. Death is a sad but inevitable part of life. It would have happened every day and, like today, no family or person is unaffected.

When Jesus saw her, his heart went out to her: "Don't cry", he said (see Luke 7:13).

With that instruction not to cry, came action. Touching the bier, he commanded the young man to get up. The dead man sat up and began to talk.

Can you imagine the tears of rejoicing the dead man's mother must have experienced at that moment? Imagine her wonder and the awe at the miracle that had just happened. How thankful she would feel for the restoration of her only son!

Our Lord Jesus did many miracles and we know them all so well. But the simple words that are recorded in this event bring tears to my eyes: "His heart went out to her" (verse 13). She hadn't asked him to do anything, but his great compassionate heart caused him to reach out and act anyway.

How awesome is this Man, our Messiah. How deeply compassionate, how loving. How many times, often at great personal expense to himself, he acts out his love, and reaches out to touch lives.

Our Lord is forgiving

Here is another encounter with Jesus. A woman who had been caught in the act of adultery was dragged before him.

The scene was obviously a set-up. The people who had brought this woman before Jesus were not so concerned about upholding the law as finding a way to trap and discredit him. With unerring wisdom, Jesus dealt with the situation masterfully. With his piercing gaze that could see into the souls of those around him, he addressed them: "Let any one of you who is without sin be the first to throw a stone at her" (John 8:7).

None of them were without sin. No one could cast the first stone. There was nothing left for them to do but leave.

"Woman, where are they? Has no one condemned you?" Jesus asked.

"No one sir", she replied.

"Then neither do I condemn you", he declared. "Go now and leave your life of sin" (John 8:10,11).

Jesus, the very one who had the power to condemn, chose not to. She was not going to feel the pain of any stone cast by Jesus that day. She was given another chance. She was given another moment to try again, to make better choices, and to respond with deep gratitude to the second chance she had been given.

She was given her life back; only "Go and sin no more".

Every new day that we live, we've been given another chance, another moment to turn our hearts in deep gratitude towards the one who has the power to forgive. Praise God for this great gift of love!

Our Lord is empathetic

If ever we want proof that our Lord Jesus is qualified to understand what we might be going through, make a careful study of his life.

Without a shadow of doubt, what the Lord went through in his life here on earth raises him above anyone who can only sympathise with us. Jesus is a man who can deeply empathise. He's been there before us; he knows what we are going through.

Listen to these descriptions, they are a sample of what Jesus suffered and endured:

He was touched with our weaknesses. He was tempted, mocked, rejected, beaten, insulted, spat upon, falsely accused, hated, humiliated, abandoned by his friends, killed by those who hated him. He was acquainted with sorrow, familiar with grief. He knew what it felt like to be without a home, to have nowhere to lay his head. He was no stranger to lack of sleep, physical exhaustion, and hunger. His cries of anguish are recorded loud and clear for us in the Psalms.

The Lord Jesus is a man who has been in the depths of the emotional pit. Any emotional experience mankind might have, he's had. He knows what it feels like; He's been there. He knows!

The Son of Man is the Son of God who has been sent into the world for our salvation and redemption from sin and death. He is righteous and fair. He is completely committed to doing what is right and just. He shows us the heart and character of his heavenly Father. His righteousness qualifies him so absolutely to be our healer and helper.

It won't be easy; and no surgery is without pain. However, a good surgeon presses on with what needs to be done, because he knows that saving a life is more important than avoiding pain!

The Lord is looking for people like me

I was out for my usual morning walk, when I saw a lady tending the plants in her front garden. She was singing to the plants, and talking to them.

I knew this lady a little. I had first encountered her when I stood behind her in a queue at a shop. She was talking to a bunch of magazines on a rack, as if they were real people. Suddenly she turned to me, and asked 'Don't you think so, lady?' I was taken aback at being drawn into the magazine conversation, and gave some lame reply, withdrawing from any further conversation. I could tell she had special needs, and I didn't know how to handle talking with her.

Thinking about it as I left the shop, I was ashamed of my inhibitions, and felt the conviction that I should have reached out and told her about Jesus.

This particular morning, as I saw her in the garden, I called out hello, and then went over to talk to her. She was delighted that I was giving her the time of day. 'Most people are scared of me', she confided, 'they think I'm mad. People mistreat me, and are mean to me.'

She showed me round her garden, telling me what type of plants she had, and what names she had given them. 'I sing to them', she said, 'they don't need anything else. They grow well when I sing and talk to them.' She insisted on giving me some flowers to take home.

As I was about to leave, she suddenly asked: 'Are you a Christian?' I affirmed that I was. She looked sad. 'I didn't grow up in a Christian home', she said. 'My parents fought, and mistreated me. I ran away from home. I was put in an Institution. The people there said they were Christian, but they mistreated me. They did terrible things to me.' I told her how sorry I was to hear about what had happened to her.

Then her face lit up. 'But I've been reading about Jesus', she said. 'You know, Jesus isn't sitting in the church pews, he's out in the highways, and the byways, down the alleys, looking for people like me. He's come to help the vile people like me!' Her eyes were bright, her face shone with the light of someone who felt loved. 'Don't you think, lady, that he's come to help vile people like me?'

My eyes were pricking with tears. I touched her arm, enclosed in a dirty jacket. 'I'm sure you're right, He has come to love people like you ... and me. Not one of us is worthy!'

'I'm doing this garden for Jesus', she confided.

'I think he will love your garden', I told her.

I left that little garden, with it's special owner, and felt again the conviction that Jesus had been visiting.

Once again, he was touching the life of one that others considered untouchable!

Our heavenly Father sent us His Son so that we could experience God's character in a tangible way. He knows us better than we know ourselves. We can have confidence to come to him with our deceitful heart because he is righteous, just, compassionate and forgiving. He knows what it's like for us to struggle with sin.

We can trust him with our heart. Not only will he be gentle and trustworthy as he deals with our deceitful hearts, but he goes far beyond the realm of any surgeon in that he also loves us more deeply than we can imagine.

Praise be to God for His wonderful gift!

> "For this people's heart has become calloused; they hardly hear with their ears, and they have closed their eyes. Otherwise they might see with their eyes, hear with their ears, understand with their hearts and turn, and I would heal them" (Matthew 13:15).

Caterpillar soup

If we were to open up a chrysalis within the first few days of it being formed, we would discover something astounding. There would be no sign of the original caterpillar. There would only be a liquid soup-like substance. If we were unaware of how the process was meant to go, we would think that something had gone terribly wrong.

But this is the way a butterfly begins. The caterpillar has first to become empty to its original form.

What an amazing process transformation is. This aspect of the process is a very vulnerable one. The creature is no longer a caterpillar; but it's not yet a butterfly either.

Keep hanging in there, little one; from what we know of how this process works, something better definitely lies ahead!

It might be uncomfortable for a while – and our next chapter takes us into the heart of an uncomfortable matter – but it is part of the process to becoming a transformed creature. Be assured, a butterfly is in the making!

In a nutshell:

- The deceit in our heart is in need of some treatment. The surgeon is trustworthy!

- Our Lord Jesus is the touchable, approachable way to understanding his Father's love for us.

- In all ways our Messiah can empathise with all our weaknesses. He loves us deeply.

- Let us turn to our Lord, with open ears, eyes, and hearts, so that he can heal us.

Prayer time:

'Heavenly Father, please open the eyes of our minds, that we might come to see how deep, how wide, and how high your love is for us. Please help us to see your love for us through the life of Jesus, your dearly loved Son. May our fears be alleviated, and help us to allow you and your Son access to our hearts, that you may come and live there. Please help us to allow you free range to do the clean-up that's needed. May we submit to your methods and your ways.
Amen.'

Chapter 14

The way of the cross

"Father, if you are willing, take this cup from me; yet not my will, but yours be done" (Luke 22:42).

"Trust in the LORD with all your heart and lean not on your own understanding; in all your ways submit to him, and he will make your paths straight" (Proverbs 3:5,6).

THERE is another way in which we are called to imitate our Lord Jesus Christ. This practice is also one that goes completely against our natural inclinations.

This action is one that requires us to relinquish our desire to be always in control.

It is the act of submission. Submitting our will to that of someone else.

I can see correlation to our yet-to-be butterfly in this action. The caterpillar has had to submit to 'diminishing in the way of self' so that it can become something more and better.

Submission for us is a platform by which we also diminish self as we prepare to let God change us. It's a difficult thing to do; and as I discovered, I revert to my natural inclinations – doing things My Way – all too often!

My way

As I stepped into the room, it became obvious to me that Robert was feeling quite upset. It was a look I've seen occasionally before, so I knew it was something to do with me; I just didn't know what.

Robert and I are not good at sharing our feelings when we are upset with each other. We usually go through our usual awkward pattern of:

'What's wrong?'

'Nothing.'

'I can tell something is wrong, what have I done?'

'I'm okay, I'll get over it …'

Finally, he revealed the source of his hurt. 'I feel like you go against everything I say. It feels like every time I express an opinion, you have an opposite one, and I end up feeling like my opinion is of no value. It makes me feel like I can never make any suggestion that you think is any good …'

I stared at him in amazement. I could think of a few instances in the last few days when I had vetoed his idea for a 'better' one, but surely it hadn't happened that often?

I asked for some clarification, and with persuasion, Robert gradually recounted the extent of his hurt, as he revealed event after event in which he had felt devalued by me.

I felt completely stunned. I had been oblivious to the fact that I had been undermining his suggestions and opinions to that extent! I have a personality that likes to be in control, and of course I always feel that I'm right! I just had been completely unaware that with every time I counteracted his wishes in favour of my own, I was eroding his sense of value. With every counter idea I had, he felt more and more disrespected.

I felt so bad that I had been pulling his sense of worth down like that. I know my husband well enough to know that, if he had come to that point of revealing his hurt, then it must be a significant thing. He doesn't generally hold on to grievances, so this must have been something that was making him feel quite dejected!

Along with this new awareness of disrespecting my husband's opinions, came a new and compelling thought. How often do I play out this same scenario with God? How often do I go against God's will, and God's direction, because 'I know better'? How often do I ignore God's ways, because I'm trusting in my own understanding? I was suddenly very sure that if I do this to my husband regularly, without being aware of it, then I must do the same to God just as often! It was a very uncomfortable thought.

Ephesians 5:22 says:

"Wives, submit to your own husbands as to the Lord" (ESV).

The concept of submission in a marriage context has caused a lot of conflict over recent years. It's definitely not in fashion! Even those like myself who pay lip service to the idea of it, may have problems with the actual application.

With the recent revelations of how disrespectful I had become of Robert's opinions, I realised how far away from submission I really was. Far away from submission to my husband, and worse still, far away from total submission to my God.

I was struck by a blinding realisation: if I can't submit to my husband, how ever do I think I'm going to be able to submit to God? Or to put it another way: practising submission to my husband, and other people, is the training ground for my submission to God.

I had missed it before now. It had gone over my head: "Wives, submit to your own husbands *as to the Lord*." If I'm submitting to the Lord, then I'm submitting to my husband.

Submitting to my husband is a part of submitting to the Lord. They go hand in hand.

What actually is submission? It's not a word we hear much of today.

The meaning of the word submission, in this context, is to yield to the will of another; to sacrifice your will to that of someone else; to give way to someone else's preference.

I think of it as submission being the attitude, and obedience being the action.

In practice, I find I can more readily give way to another's will if their idea isn't too far off track with my own. However, if their idea is way out of synch with mine, then I automatically voice opposition. To practise submission means not only to give way to someone else's preference, but to do it without any black grudging looks.

The Bible outlines a number of different scenarios that require a submissive attitude. We are all asked to submit to authorities, because they have been placed over us. Slaves are asked to submit to their masters, with all respect – whether the masters are good or harsh. Wives are asked to submit to their husbands, as to the Lord. We are all asked to submit to each other, out of reverence for Christ.

The Bible shows us that submitting is an attitude of love, given freely out of respect for God and Christ.

Your will, not mine

Our Lord Jesus has, once again, shown us what submission looks like. He submitted to his Father in everything. He and his Father were on the same page. Jesus submitted his way to his Father all the way through. Well, I thought, that was easy for him, he was completely in agreement with his Father, and with his Father's methods. He didn't disagree with any of his Father's way or plans.

Until I remembered the road to the cross. "Abba, Father", he said, "everything is possible for you. Take this cup from me" (Mark 14:36). No, all was not straightforward and easy for Jesus. With all his heart, he wanted this cup, this way, to be taken from him. If only another way were possible. God's pathway for Jesus led to the cross. It was painful, big, and hard. 'Is there no other way, Father?'

"Yet not what I will, but what you will."

It was hard, but Jesus submitted to the way of the cross, even though he really did not want to.

"Not my will, but yours be done." Thinking about it, Jesus' whole life on earth was filled with little acts of submission.

- 'I'm really tired, I would just like some rest now. Oh no, here come some more people, they want me to heal them.'

    "Not my will, but yours be done."

- 'They think I'm mad, that I've lost my mind. I would like to show them; just a little show of power ...?'

    "Not my will, but yours be done."

- 'I've been up all day, healing, teaching, showing love. I really need some sleep and rest. But what about prayer time with my Father? All night?'

    "Not my will, but yours be done."

- 'I'm hungry, I would just love to make myself some bread out of these stones. I can, I have the power ...'

    "Not my will, but yours be done."

- 'Forgive them? Really?'

    "Not my will, but yours be done."

- 'I could come down from this cross, and show them that I am the Son of God.'

    "Not my will, but yours be done!"

Continual daily acts of submission to his Father's way of doing things paved the way for that final act of submission right to the end. Constant daily alignment to his Father's will empowered him to sacrifice his own will in favour of a higher and more noble way. A way of pain, certainly. But overall, it was the way of triumph and victory. Sin and death were defeated on this pathway. This was a cause for celebration, and great joy. The way of the cross – submission to his Father's will – had the last and final laugh.

Submitting our will

Submitting to the Lord, and His ways, is an essential part of our relationship with Him. Submission requires trust and belief. It requires us to let go of our own understanding, and to lean on the Lord. It means that we acknowledge that His way is the best way, even when it doesn't make sense to us.

In the same way, trust is required for us to submit to the ministrations of a surgeon. We know that the surgeon has our best interests in mind, and has the intention of fixing whatever problem we have. A short season of pain in this process is for the benefit of long-term gain.

We know we need to submit to a surgeon in a practical and physical sense. But with matters that relate to the heart, and our personal sense of value, it's so much harder!

This is why we have other people in our lives to practise on. This is why God has asked us to live lives of submission to each other. He knows we need the practice, because submitting to Him doesn't come naturally!

What does submission look like in our day-to-day lives?

Submission to a husband

If we are married, then our husband is the first person we get to practise on!

Here are a few scenarios we may encounter that could give us some practice at submission:

- **He's suggesting this activity. I don't really feel like it, but is it really going to hurt that much to do it?** ('Okay, sure, we can do that.')

- **He thinks it should be done this way. But I think my way is better!** (But really, will it be the end of the world if I try his suggestion?)

- **He wants me to do this for him. I don't really want to ...** ('Sure, I can do this for you. Do you want it done now, or would a little later be okay?')

- **I disagree with what he has just said.** (Does he need to be corrected, or am I really just sweating the small stuff?)

There are also submission opportunities for us in responding to our husband's sexual needs; showing him respect; speaking his 'love language'; following up on ways to serve and give.

Submitting to other people

The other people in our lives provide us with plenty of opportunities to practise submission, grace and love. This applies within an ecclesial setting, as well as the neighbourhood around us. Frequently, it's hard to do. Pride gets in the way. Fatigue and disinclination play a part. Time and inconvenience are major factors. But each little step we take towards following in Jesus' footsteps, and sacrificing our will in favour of another's, we grow that much closer to the submissive attitude God wants us to have.

Let's think about our reactions and responses to some particular situations we might find ourselves in.

How do we react or respond to other people when:

- We disagree, and feel a burning desire to let them know they are wrong ...?

- A person has upset us, and we feel hurt ...?

- We want recognition, to be appreciated, to have a moment to shine; but rather we feel ignored and unappreciated ...?

- Someone is expressing their view; we disagree, and we want to correct or refute ...?

- We are challenged in our viewpoint ...?

- Someone acts in a hurtful way ...?

Opportunities to submit to other people also include acts of service; responding to needs; turning the other cheek; going the extra mile; blessing those who curse; praying for those who hurt us; finding ways to do good and be helpful; being a blessing.

Submitting to God

"And this is love: that we walk in obedience to his commands" (2 John verse 6).

God's Word gives us a lot of instruction about conduct and way of life. It gives us many submission opportunities. Familiarity may find us becoming indifferent, making excuses, or giving ourselves wriggle room with them. Fully submitting to God's commands sometimes looks blurry around the edges, or even non-existent. I know that is certainly true for me!

Here are some submission opportunities:

- **Listen and obey.** Do we sometimes excuse ourselves from obeying parts of God's Word because 'it's not relevant to us today' or 'that's not what it really means, when it says ...'? Do we follow through on the prompts that come our way: to give, to do, to speak up, to refrain from speaking, to apologise, to give something up?

- **Trust and belief.** How do we respond to those moments when life doesn't make sense, when we can't see why God has allowed a certain situation? Are we letting go, and letting God take control? Does worry threaten to overcome trust? Does doubt, pain or fear overwhelm faith? Do we believe we can be forgiven? Do we believe there is a hope and a future for us?

- **Love God with all our heart, soul, mind and strength.** Are we letting God into our lives, even in the no-go areas that we don't want anyone to pry into? Are we willing to give the Lord every area of our lives, our whole body, mind and heart?

Opportunities to submit to God revolve around obedience, love, faith and trust. Putting Him in number one place in our lives is of first importance to Him. Trusting and believing that He has our best interests at heart is an important part of submitting to Him.

"Not my will, but yours be done ..."

Sacrificing our will to someone else's will is one of the hardest things we can do. If it were easy, it would no longer be a sacrifice. Living out small daily acts of sacrifice certainly helps with the ability to submit in the bigger things of life.

Accept or excuse?

A parable that our Lord Jesus told gives us a stark contrast between our way and the Lord's way. This parable shows that despite having been given the most amazing offer of a lifetime, it's incredibly easy to pass it up because we are too focused on our own agenda!

"A certain man was preparing a great banquet and invited many guests. At the time of the banquet he sent his servant to tell those who had been invited, 'Come, for everything is now ready.' But they all alike began to make excuses. The first said, 'I have just bought a field, and I must go and see it. Please excuse me.' Another said, 'I have just bought five yoke of oxen, and I'm on my way to try them out. Please excuse me.' Still another said, 'I just got married, so I can't come'" (Luke 14:16-20).

The end result of their excuses was not a good one.

"I tell you, not one of those who were invited will get a taste of my banquet" (verse 24).

One day, the time will come when we no longer have the opportunity for submission. The time to practise "not my will, but yours be done", is right now. When the time for the banquet comes, if we have not practised sacrificing our will now, we may find that we have turned down the most amazing banquet ever, for a pile of excuses!

Submitting is part of the process of allowing God to transform our deceitful, stony hearts into hearts that love and respond to Him. Submission is a necessary part of transformation. It requires us to diminish ourselves, and to bend our will to another's.

Submission is beautifully summed up in the sentiments our Lord Jesus took on in Psalm 40:

"Then I said, 'Here I am, I have come – it is written about me in the scroll. I desire to do your will, my God'; your law is within my heart" (verses 7,8).

Our Lord Jesus desired to do his Father's will!

As I think back to the process that is going on inside the chrysalis, I can acknowledge that, as unpleasant as it all seems, it is a necessary part of transformation. The caterpillar needs to submit to being reduced to the soup state, so that it can become something more and better.

Now is our opportunity. A new, clean, heart can only be achieved if we submit to the methods of the surgeon. "Not my will, but yours be done."

This is the way of the cross.

In a nutshell:

- Diminishing self, and submitting our will to God is a necessary part of transformation.

- The training ground for that to happen comes through our human relationships.

- Our Lord Jesus has shown us the way with his submission to his Father, in everything. Especially in submitting to death on the cross.

- "Not my will, but yours be done."

Prayer time:

Let us pray that we can grow our desire to do God's will, and to submit to His ways.

Personal note

When I wrote my personalised wedding vows, I deliberately left out the promise to obey my husband; mostly because I didn't think I could live up to it. That was a true observation; even if it was a bit of a cop out!

What I had never previously considered, however, was the direct correlation between living a life of submission to other people, and submitting to God. I suppose I thought that submission to other people was slightly optional, dependent on the other person's idea being in line with my own! On the other hand, I had always assumed that I was trying to submit to God, and was attempting obedience of His ways. So the realisation that I was actually no better at submitting to God than I was at submitting to my human relationships was an eye-opener. I had not seen how connected the two are. Submitting to God was going to be best achieved when I practised it daily with the other people in my life.

Sacrificing my will and my way to someone else's has been a hard thing for me to do. It's still a work in progress.

Proverbs 3:5 tells us that to trust God means that we can't lean on our own understanding. I'm adept at leaning on my own understanding, but poor at trusting God. Sacrificing my will is a trust moment: will I trust God with the outcome, or will I carry on with my way?

Being aware of my trust and submission problem has become a vital step towards change, so I'm grateful for that.

Meanwhile, my husband is graciously willing to allow me to practise on him!

Chapter 15

A right spirit

"Create in me a clean heart, O God, and renew a right spirit within me" (Psalm 51:10, ESV).

"I will give you a new heart and put a new spirit in you; I will remove from you your heart of stone and give you a heart of flesh" (Ezekiel 36:26).

"Good and upright is the LORD; therefore he instructs sinners in his ways. He guides the humble in what is right and teaches them his way" (Psalm 25:8,9).

WE are well aware by now that we have a deceitful heart. It is in our heart where the change needs to begin.

It will require effort for us to gain a new, clean heart, and a right spirit. Our Lord Jesus has been sent by our heavenly Father to walk alongside us through this process. He has shown us the way, been the example, and is very qualified to be the facilitator of the changes that are needed!

All of this is moving us toward our value increasing in the sight of God; incredible as it sounds!

Once we are willing to empty ourselves, and allow the Lord to work on our hearts, we will then be ready to find out what needs to change within us.

To help us along with the process of heart change, God has left us with instructions as to how we can live in obedience to Him. Psalm 25 tells us that the Lord instructs sinners in His ways, and guides the humble in what is right.

We know that God speaks to us directly through His Word. His Word is our source of direction and enlightenment. It's a Must to read if we want to know His ways better!

He also sends us prompts and nudges through a variety of ways. We just need to have our eyes, ears and hearts open to them! We need a humble spirit to be able to listen to God, as the Psalmist says.

A humble spirit

A humble spirit is one that allows us to hear and respond to God. Humility works alongside submission. It is the number one way to let go of self. Humility requires us to lean not on our own understanding, but to lean on God.

Humility is another really hard attitude to cultivate!

I know I find humility hard. Frequently I find myself leaning on my own understanding, and reverting to defensiveness and self-justification.

However, humility is what God is asking of us, so it must be important to work toward it.

It's worth reminding ourselves about what the Bible says about humility, and why God thinks it's important for us:

"Who is wise and understanding among you? Let them show it by their good life, by deeds done in the humility that comes from wisdom" (James 3:13).

"Humble yourselves before the Lord, and he will lift you up" (4:10).

"He scorns the scornful, but gives grace to the humble" (Proverbs 3:34, NKJV).

These verses tell us that wisdom forms the foundation for humility. The verses tell us that practising humility enables God to lift us up. They also inform us that grace is bestowed on those who cultivate a humble spirit.

All of these are very motivating factors to encourage humility in us.

People provide us with great opportunity for humility training! As we contemplated previously with submission, the ways in which we respond to the people that annoy us, set us up for how we respond to God.

Being prepared to learn from other people, and listen to them, is a great way to begin cultivating a humble spirit.

Our son Jeremy told me of a time at work when he had an opportunity for a good humility workout. He was an apprentice for an electrical company. One of the tradesmen there had a habit of provoking Jeremy, needling and make disparaging comments. This one particular day he was watching Jeremy work, and his critical comments were frustrating Jeremy intensely.

Jeremy eventually stopped responding to him, and pointedly ignored the critical comments. This frustrated the co-worker, who now felt disrespected by Jeremy.

Later, as Jeremy thought it through, he decided he would go and apologise for not responding. He summoned his courage, and went to find his co-worker so that he could apologise. What a wise action to take. The apology helped deflate a situation that could have become fuel for ongoing rancour.

Humility in our responses to people, and humility before God, are essential elements to maintaining a soft and pliable heart. Humility is not a sign of weakness, as some might think.

On the contrary, humility requires a great strength of character and a willingness to let God be the judge of any given situation.

At this point, it's worth asking the question: do we always have to back down before people? Is that what humility, or even submission, is all about? Is it always about giving way to others? What about when we believe they are wrong in their treatment of us, or wrong in their requirements?

The apostles in the book of Acts give us some useful insights of how to respond in these sort of situations. The apostles had been out preaching and healing, doing all in the name of Jesus. As a result, they were thrown into prison and reprimanded by the leaders of the Jews. They were given strict orders to stop teaching and healing in Jesus' name.

Peter spoke on their behalf, and said: "We must obey God rather than men!" (Acts 5:29, ESV).

Sometimes man's requirements are at variance with God's requirements. This will mean that we may respectfully decline what man might be asking of us.

At other times, the things that people ask of us are not necessarily at variance with God, but they don't sit right with our judgement or understanding. In this case, some prayerful consideration as to how we respond might be a good call. Whether we choose to submit to the situation, or whether we decline, it must be done with a respect that shows humility and understanding.

Another question: how do we learn to be humble? Philippians 2 has some helpful thoughts.

> "Do nothing from selfish ambition or conceit, but in humility count others more significant than yourselves. Let each of you look not only to his own interests, but also to the interests of others" (verses 3,4, ESV).

"Do everything without grumbling or arguing" (verse 14).

Viewing others as a loved child of God, and being mindful of their interests are great attitudes for learning humility.

This is not to say that we are of 'less value' than anyone else, but being considerate of their needs will help us keep self in perspective.

Above all, let's stay on our knees, asking for help to respond to God, and to others, in ways that can grow our humility, and honour God.

A humble spirit is the only way in which we will be able to 'hear' God speak to us about being off track with Him. I mean really hear, in an understanding sort of way! Humility is the only way we're going to be able to respond positively to the changes that need to be made in our lives.

So now, with awareness of our need for humility let's consider some other ways God might help us become aware of the deceit in our hearts.

God's Word

"My son [daughter], if you accept my words and store up my commands within you, turning your ear to wisdom and applying your heart to understanding ... and if you look for it as for silver and search for it as for hidden treasure, then you will understand the fear of the LORD and find the knowledge of God. For the LORD gives wisdom; from his mouth come knowledge and understanding" (Proverbs 2:1-6).

God speaks to us constantly through His Word, showing us the right way, and warning us of the way that is wrong. We need to ask Him to speak to us through His Word, to gain wisdom and insight for each day and throughout our lives. We then need to allow Him to work in our hearts through the scripture we have read.

A great prayer for the start of our Bible reading time is to ask God to show us the message that is there for us that day. We can pray that He will help us to see what is particularly pertinent for us in that moment.

As we read His Scripture, we can ask that our minds and hearts might be opened to what stirs our heart, or what pricks or provokes our conscience. Is there a command to obey, or a behaviour to change? Is there a reassurance to take on board? Is there a call to trust and believe? Are we being instructed about things to let go, or things to embrace? Is there a reminder of forgiveness to extend or receive?

Then we should meditate on the words and verses that speak strongly to us, and allow them to expand and grow in our minds; to facilitate changes in our heart.

"All scripture is God-breathed and is useful for teaching, rebuking, correcting and training in righteousness, so that the servant of God may be thoroughly equipped for every good work" (2 Timothy 3:16,17).

Asking God

The third way we can listen to God, to grow a right spirit, is to ask God specifically about where we might be out of step with Him. The benefits of this are immense, if we are prepared to listen and allow God to open awareness in our heart.

David invited God to do this in Psalm 139:

"Search me, O God, and know my heart; test me and know my anxious thoughts. See if there is any offensive way in me, and lead me in the way everlasting" (verses 23,24).

David recognised that God is infinitely the best judge of character and motives. According to the sentiments in this psalm, David was not leaving revelation of offensive ways to chance; he invited God to search his heart, and to lead him in the right way.

A number of years ago, for the first time in my life, I included a confession element to my prayer time. This involved confessing to God the areas of my life in which I had noticed I was falling short. I asked forgiveness for these, and asked for help to overcome.

After that, I asked the Lord if there were other areas of my life that I was off track, and that I was unaware of. This was a particularly eye-opening experience. I marvel at how blind I am to my own shortcomings!

After inviting God to be part of this process, I started to become aware of how pride was operating in my life. This was surprising to me, because I had not previously considered myself to be a particularly prideful person. I started to see how comparing myself to others had its root in pride. How envying others was pride, how false humility was based in pride, how my critical judgemental attitude could be traced back to pride. Even allowing myself to feel overly hurt by criticism was a form of pride.

Pride, I discovered, was insidious. Pride was at the root of many of my negative attitudes. It is also one of the things that God hates most. It's a primary symptom of a deceitful heart.

I was grateful for the new awareness of something that I had previously been oblivious to. I was grateful for God's great love. He doesn't want any of us to be permanently off track with Him. He wants us to be aware of our sins and weaknesses, so that we can turn to Him for healing. This is really awe-inspiring!

Unfortunately, I don't always make the effort to ask. I am in a hurry. It's not a 'fun' thing to do. So I frequently neglect this very important step.

But it is needful; so in this I encourage myself, as well as you, to ask God for help so that our eyes may be open to where we are off track with Him.

Messages through people

"In those days John the Baptist came, preaching in the wilderness of Judea and saying, 'Repent, for the kingdom of heaven has come near'" (Matthew 3:1,2).

John the Baptist came with a pretty punchy message for the people of his day. He didn't wrap his words up in cotton wool. "You brood of vipers" was one of the unflattering descriptions he used of the people who came to hear his message.

Not surprisingly, there was mixed response to John's message.

Those who were humble enough to receive his message favourably, asked: "What should we do then?" To them, John exhorted, encouraged and preached a message of repentance.

The other group of people did not respond favourably. One of these was Herod. His reaction to John's message was to lock John up in prison. Herod did not hear, see, or understand John's message. He did not turn from his sinful actions so that he could be healed.

The Bible is full of examples, like John, of God sending messages through people. The prophets were sent to speak God's words of warning and of repentance. The Lord Jesus came to be God's word made flesh.

The young man Timothy was given this instruction from Paul:

"Preach the word, be prepared in season and out of season; correct, rebuke and encourage – with great patience and careful instruction" (2 Timothy 4:2).

God will use people to encourage, rebuke or correct us. Let's pause, before we react defensively, to consider whether the message we are receiving might contain some godly wisdom. It's worth considering what we might be able to learn from what others say.

I recall an unusual encounter I had during a supermarket shopping trip one day. Our daughter Charis was only a toddler at the time. In my memory, it was a relatively calm shopping day. I don't remember Charis having any particularly cranky moments, or me having any particularly exasperated-mother moments. I was scanning the shelves when a stranger approached me. 'Excuse me', he said, 'Your daughter is a very sensitive child, you need to be very careful how you handle her.'

I was taken aback with his out-of-the-blue statement, and only had enough wits about me to thank him before he disappeared around another aisle. But his warning has stayed with me through the years as Charis has grown. At that point in her young life, I hadn't noticed the signs of sensitivity in my daughter, but I have certainly come to see it as she has got older. Whether this instruction was specifically God-sent, or whether it was only an observation from a very perceptive stranger, I have none-the-less taken his suggestion on board and have been trying to handle her sensitivity carefully.

Let's listen with humility to the encouragement, rebuke and correction that we might receive from other people. Let's pray that God will reveal any wisdom that we should take from those encounters.

Our conscience

God sends nudges to us through our conscience. Our conscience may prick us at times, telling us that we are out of line and that something needs to change. Our conscience can only be activated, and works best, if our understanding of God's ways is sharpened through regular reading of His Word, and not weakened by exposure to dubious things.

I know how easy it is to dull the responses of my conscience. I grew up in a home that did not have a television. So, when I watched anything as a young adult, my conscience was very strong about telling me what was inappropriate. I recall being in a situation where I was watching a few movies with a group of other people. One of the movies contained content that made me feel very uncomfortable. My conscience was pricking me loud and clear: this was not appropriate material to be watching!

Once I left home and got married, we had a television in our home for a while. After some time of having regular exposure to the various programmes on offer, my conscience became dull. I no longer had the same violent disgust of things that I would once have considered inappropriate to watch.

We need to be very careful that we are not dulling our conscience with exposure to immorality and evil. If we do, our conscience will no longer work in our favour. We will become desensitised.

Let us listen to our conscience, and be willing to initiate change if we find we have wandered off God's pathway.

God may also send us prompts through our subconscious. The subconscious mind is fuelled by what has been fed to the conscious mind. So where the conscience has been activated by knowledge of right and wrong, the subconscious can step in and work almost on autopilot.

I would call it a 'light bulb' moment. The prodigal son, in Jesus' parable, experienced a light bulb moment. As his life came crashing round his ears and he found himself having to feed pigs to survive, he came to a stunning revelation:

"When he came to his senses, he said, 'How many of my father's hired servants have food to spare, and here I am starving to death! I will set out and go back to my father and say to him: Father, I have sinned against heaven and against you. I am no longer worthy to be called your son; make me like one of your hired servants'" (Luke 15:17-19).

How many times might similar moments happen for us? We are blindly going our own way, and then a sudden realisation pops into our mind, and we too 'come to our senses'! If, on reflection, we find we are spending far too much time 'with the pigs', we need to be able to respond to those prompts, like the prodigal son did, and turn back to our Father.

'Light bulb' moments will look different for each person. God knows what will work best for each of us. The point is, we need to have hearts, minds, ears and eyes that are open to receiving the prompts. When we get them, let us thank God for them, and be prepared to follow through with whatever might need to change!

Above all, we need to keep feeding our minds with the Word of God, so that our conscience or even subconscious has a chance to reflect the ways of God back to us.

Through our circumstances

David was furious. He had spent a lot of time and resources looking out for Nabal's livestock while he and his men camped around Nabal's property. When David's men had approached Nabal with a request for food and drink, David expected that Nabal would treat them favourably.

But Nabal was a hard-hearted, callous man, and he responded rudely to David's request, sending David's men away empty-handed.

David was thoroughly riled by this treatment. He said:

"May God deal with David, be it ever so severely, if by morning I leave alive one male of all who belong to him!" (1 Samuel 25:22).

However, Nabal's wife, Abigail, was a very wise woman. She jumped into action with a gift of food, and humbly approached David to plead for mercy. She went out of her way to avert the disaster that was about to come upon her household.

Listen to her words to David:

"Since the LORD has kept you from bloodshed and from avenging yourself with your own hands, may your enemies and all who are intent on harming my Lord be like Nabal" (verse 26).

David replied:

"Praise be to the LORD, the God of Israel, who has sent you today to meet me. May you be blessed for your good judgment and for keeping me from bloodshed this day and from avenging myself with my own hands. Otherwise, as surely as the LORD, the God of Israel, lives, who has kept me from harming you, if you had not come quickly to meet me, not one male belonging to Nabal would have been left alive by daybreak" (verses 32-34).

David and Abigail both recognised God's hand at work in keeping David from vengeful bloodshed. While Abigail was the tool through which it would happen, God was the mastermind behind the operation.

How many times does God work through the circumstances of our lives, engineering events, to enable us to have the best chance of making a right choice? I suspect there are more than we are aware of, and many more than we might give Him credit for!

Humility also came into play in this drama. David needed to be humble enough to accept the gift offered, and to relinquish the right to vengeance.

Abigail had to be humble enough to shoulder the responsibility of smoothing over the trouble that her husband had caused.

My husband Robert recalls moments where he has felt thankful to God for interruptions that have come at opportune moments. He recalls one instance where he was just a click away from opening some inappropriate material on the computer. As his hand hovered over the button, the phone rang. The moment of temptation was broken with him needing to answer the phone. He was able to walk away from the temptation, and he was thankful to God for the providential diversion.

Let's learn to be aware of God working in the circumstances of our lives. Through our circumstances, He allows us opportunity, time and time again, to align ourselves with His way.

Review

A great way to finish off any day, and to open our mind to the awareness of God's hand in our lives, is to do a review of the day's events.

The use of a journal is really beneficial for this. As the day ends, we can ask God to help us scan the day in our mind, seeking awareness of where we might have been out of line. Have we spent time with God today? Have we spoken any unwise words? Have we reacted with impatience or anger? Have we missed opportunities? Reflecting on our day with an open mind, seeking awareness, helps our eyes to be opened to where we've been off track in any area. Writing it down helps to crystallise our thoughts and promotes awareness of things that might need change or help. This time of reflection can then form the basis of a prayer for forgiveness, help and healing. What a beautiful way to conclude the day. Sleep can be sweet with the knowledge of forgiveness, given at the asking.

"Search me, God, and know my heart ... see if there is any offensive way in me."

"Create in me a clean heart"

God wants us to be aware of where we are out of step with Him. There are many ways that He helps open our eyes to what is going on in our lives. We know that God speaks to us through

His Word. But there are other prompts and nudges that might help us along the way as well. Cultivating a humble spirit will help open our heart to receive those messages and prompts. When our heart is open and receptive, our eyes and ears will be able to see, hear and understand. We will be able to turn to God for healing.

May we also be willing to echo David's words in this prayer: "Create in me a clean heart, O God, and renew a right spirit within me" (Psalm 51:10).

With this as our attitude, we will be on the road toward trust, submission to God's ways, and obedience.

As we conclude this chapter, we will take another virtual look inside the chrysalis. It's still pretty liquid in there. No caterpillar, and, as yet, no butterfly.

It is interesting to learn that within the liquid substance in the chrysalis, there are still cells that are from the caterpillar. Some of the original tissue will pass on to the butterfly's body. This will form the basis of the new wings, antennae and legs.

It's exciting to think that God can do a similar thing for us, if we let Him. He can take some of our original material and turn it into something that is radically different, but very beautiful!

A clean heart, and a right spirit, is the place where it all begins.

In a nutshell:

- God wants us to be aware of the ways we are off track with Him. He provides us with instruction through His Word. He may also send prompts and nudges our way to help us make the right choices.

- A humble spirit is needed to help us receive teaching, correction, instruction, rebuke and training in righteousness.

- People are a great training ground for us, to help us grow humility!

Prayer time:

"Create in me a clean heart, O God, and renew a right spirit within me."

Chapter 16

Confession

"If we confess our sins, he is faithful and just and will forgive us our sins and purify us from all unrighteousness. If we claim we have not sinned, we make him out to be a liar and his word is not in us" (1 John 1:9,10).

"Therefore confess your sins to each other and pray for each other so that you may be healed. The prayer of a righteous man is powerful and effective" (James 5:16).

INSIDE the chrysalis fluid, substance was beginning to form. As the days passed, a butterfly was starting to take shape. Gradually, wings and body were becoming discernible. As the time went on, the chrysalis was changing colour. It was becoming a deeper shade of green. The changes to the outside colouring indicated that change was going on inside. This is heartening to see, and it shows that it won't be too much longer before a newly transformed butterfly is ready to be revealed!

We are also at the point of further action in our transformation journey.

From the time we become aware of having deceit in our heart, we have been given the choice either to acknowledge it or hide it.

When we choose to acknowledge the deceit in our heart, we open it up to healing and change. When we open our heart to change, we agree to submit to the way of the Surgeon. Fortunately, we know that our Surgeon is faithful, just and trustworthy. He is willing to forgive our sins and purify us from all unrighteousness.

In much the same way as a chrysalis deepens in colour to indicate that change is happening, confession is a significant marker for us in our journey of transformation.

Acknowledgement

A man was sent to confront King David (the man after God's own heart), with the enormity of his sin after his affair with Bathsheba.

Nathan approached David in a clever manner. He told David a story.

The story was about two men. One was rich, the other poor. The rich man had many sheep and cattle, but the poor man had only one little ewe lamb. This little ewe lamb meant the world to him, it even slept in his arms. When a traveller arrived at the rich man's home, the rich man did not take one of his own animals to prepare a meal for the visitor. He instead took the little ewe lamb that belonged to his poor neighbour.

As you can imagine, David was incensed by the callous act of the rich man. He was really angry at this selfishness. He declared that the one who had done such a thing deserved to die!

He waited expectantly for Nathan to reveal the perpetrator of this crime.

'You are that man, David ...'

How many people throughout history, when confronted with their sin, responded favourably toward those who revealed it to them?

We have already considered what Herod did to John, when John confronted him about taking his brother's wife. We have already thought about the response the leaders of the day had towards Jesus.

The end result was pretty ugly. There was no listening, no receiving of the message, and no softening of the heart. There was no confession, no repentance, and no healing.

David chose a different response:

"Have mercy on me, O God, according to your unfailing love; according to your great compassion blot out my transgressions. Wash away all my iniquity and cleanse me from my sin. For I know my transgressions, and my sin is always before me. Against you, you only, have I sinned and done what is evil in your sight" (Psalm 51:1-4).

David accepted his guilt. He acknowledged his sin. He repented of what he had done. He was teachable and humble enough to receive the reprimand. His heart was soft and pliable; making him a perfect candidate for heart surgery.

"Create in me a clean heart ... renew a right spirit within me" (verse 10, ESV).

What about us? Are we prepared to choose to acknowledge and confess our sin, as David did? Will we listen to the prompts and nudges that come our way? What will we do when we become aware of the way our hearts have deceived us?

The Lord wants us to choose the pathway of confession and repentance. It is what David chose. It is the only way that our hearts can be healed and made clean. Confession and repentance are our next step of action after we become aware of whatever way deceit is operating in our heart.

Some of the ways our hearts deceive us are obvious – the big, out there, visible sins of commission.

Others are less visible; just quietly, deceitfully nibbling away at our character. The gossip, anger, pride, envy, self-righteousness, self-justification, defensiveness ...

Some of them are just tiny seeds of deceitful attitude. But we can't leave them unchecked. They will grow!

I remember seeing a school production about a plant that grew into something nasty. It started out as a 'harmless' little thing. It was fed and watered, and it grew steadily larger. It was greatly admired in the flower shop where it resided. But this plant had a carnivorous appetite. For it to grow, it needed flesh to eat. The bigger it got, the greater its appetite. Its owner didn't know what to do. On the one hand he was rather fond of his plant. On the other hand, its appetite was getting out of control.

In the end, the owner was 'owned' by the plant. The plant's demands dictated this man's life.

As I recall, it didn't have a 'happily ever after ending'. It was not a feel-good story!

But it has a lot of resemblance to what our lives can look like with sin dictating how we live. Unless we can say, 'I've had enough of this – I am no longer going to be ruled by this!', we end up being 'owned' by the growing plant of deceit!

Confession

"If we confess our sins, he is faithful and just and will forgive us our sins and purify us from all unrighteousness" (1 John 1:9).

David knew the process. Once he had been confronted with the enormity of his sin, he came clean. You might think that he would already be well aware that he had done wrong. Adultery and murder are considered two of the more heavy-weight sins, even today. But that is how easy it is for us to justify our actions, and to ignore the sin that is in our lives!

Listen to how he felt before he owned up to and acknowledged the guilt of his actions:

"... When I kept silent, my bones wasted away through my groaning all day long. For day and night your hand was heavy on me; my strength was sapped as in the heat of summer" (Psalm 32:3,4).

But then with his confession, came relief:

"Then I acknowledged my sin to you and did not cover up my iniquity. I said, 'I will confess my transgressions to the LORD.' And you forgave the guilt of my sin'" (verse 5).

What a weight must have been removed from David at that point. How much lighter in spirit and soul he would have felt. He confessed. He was forgiven. How beautiful is that!

One of my children experienced a moment of relief brought about by confession. It turned out that my small child had given in to the temptation of shop-lifting. It was just little trinkets from the $2 shop; but it was stealing all the same. I was unaware of this, until one night a tearful child confessed to the crime. It had been eating away at their conscience for a while, creating a similar feeling to what David described. I think it might have brought about a few sleepless nights too!

The relief of confessing was big. It was not an easy thing to do, but it was worth the relief it produced. There were consequences, of course. We had to return the items, and admit to the shopkeeper what had happened. But it was still worth the relief of coming clean.

Confession, and asking forgiveness, can also help break the sin cycle.

A wise brother in Christ, who is also a counsellor, gave some extremely helpful advice for dealing with addictive problems that lead to us repeatedly giving in to temptation.

He said, that every time we give in to temptation and sin, we should always confess, say sorry, and ask forgiveness. Even if it happens every day. Eventually, he said, something will stop. Either we stop saying sorry, and asking forgiveness, or we stop the behaviour. It gets embarrassing to have to keep saying sorry for the same thing over and over, so eventually something has to change in our behaviour!

Don't give up on confession, he advised, it is the best move to make towards overcoming.

Confess, out loud. Be specific. Express remorse. Ask for forgiveness.

Confession is the pathway that leads to victory and healing.

Our confession doesn't stop with God, however. There will be times that we need to confess, and ask forgiveness of other people; especially if they have been on the receiving end of something we have done or said.

This can be much harder than saying sorry to God. We can't see God. We can see people.

However, God knows that our healing is going to be most effective when we confess openly to the person affected by our sins.

Confession requires courage. It also requires humility. These are two factors that might need some earnest prayer from us!

One speaker termed it: 'Three magic phrases', 'I am sorry. I was wrong (for) ... Please forgive me.'

Even if no one else is directly affected by our shortcomings, there is still amazing healing that can be gained by sharing our problem with another (trustworthy) person.

Confessing to other people allows opportunity for someone else to pray for us and hurt with us. They can partner with us in the healing process, and walk alongside us to give us support.

Active confession – to God and others – is a vital step in our heart healing process.

Active confession is vital for transformation. It's like the part in the chrysalis process where the chrysalis is changing colour. It's getting ready for the butterfly to emerge.

This is part of the process of decreasing ourselves, so that God can give us the increase.

Forgiveness

"Blessed is he whose transgression is forgiven, whose sin is covered. Blessed is the man to whom the LORD does not impute iniquity, and in whose spirit there is no deceit" (Psalm 32:1,2, NKJV).

What a beautiful place to be: not perfect, but forgiven! This was David's experience. He had gone through the agonising process of awareness, acknowledgement and repentance. Finally he arrived at forgiven. A clean heart, a right spirit.

Forgiven is the place that baptism brings us to. It is where the sin slate is wiped clean, and robes of righteousness are given to us.

Forgiven is the place we arrive at every time we confess, repent and ask to be forgiven.

The person with a pliable heart, who can receive rebuke, and repent, will experience this amazing gift.

It is a most beautiful thing to be forgiven, washed and made clean again. Past sins are put behind, buried at the bottom of the sea, and cast from east to west! Such is the language of the Bible, showing how God discards the sins that we have handed over to Him. This is how beautifully loving our Father is to us. He no longer holds our sins against us. What a precious gift!

God doesn't have a limit on how much forgiveness He is prepared to give out either. Our Lord Jesus said that we should be prepared to forgive each other 70 × 7 times in a day if we are asked. The Lord is not asking of us anything that He would not be prepared to do himself!

That's a lot of forgiveness. That's a lot of asking!

Pressing on

Forgiveness cannot be taken for granted, or used as a back-stop for deliberate sin. We are no longer who we were. We are no longer 'owned' by the nasty plant of sin. Neither are we shackled to the guilt of past misdemeanours. Forgiveness gives us freedom.

To keep himself from being pulled down by the sins of his past, the Apostle Paul used this strategy:

> "Not that I have already obtained all this, or have already arrived at my goal, but I press on to take hold of that for which Christ Jesus took hold of me ... But one thing I do: Forgetting what is behind and straining toward what is ahead, I press on toward the goal to win the prize for which God has called me heavenward in Christ Jesus" (Philippians 3:12-14).

Paul was not going to allow the past to pull him back. Whatever was in the past, was going to stay there. He had learnt from it, but it was not going to be allowed to pull him backwards with guilt. Instead he was intent with pressing on toward the goal and straining on towards what lay ahead. He was focused on living life fully for that moment and beyond.

The past (and there were a lot of guilt-worthy moments from his past), had to be put behind him, so that he could live usefully in the present.

As we press on towards our goal of transformation, let us take up the challenge. This challenge is to go deeper in our change process where transformation can really change us. It requires us to be open to the awareness of sin in our lives. To acknowledge our sin. To repent. To be forgiven. To press on.

May the grace of our Lord be with us throughout this process.

In a nutshell:

- Awareness of deceit in our heart gives us opportunity to respond through confession and repentance.

- We need to confess both to God and other people.

- Forgiveness washes our sins away, and gives us a clean start.

- Forgiveness gives us opportunity to 'forget the past, and press on towards what is ahead'.

Prayer time:

Let us pray that our hearts are not hard, and that our eyes and ears are open to our heart's deceit. Let us ask that we might 'see with our eyes, hear with our ears, understand with our hearts, and turn, and be healed.'

Chapter 17

The gift of grace

'Be assured', the Lord said, 'My ways you can trust,
Look to Jesus, follow him, be like him, it's a must!
Come to know him, and see just how great is my love,
For through him I offer you grace from above!'

"See what great love the Father has lavished on us, that we should be called children of God! And that is what we are!" (1 John 3:1).

"This is how we know what love is: Jesus Christ laid down his life for us" (verse 16).

ALONGSIDE forgiveness, our amazing God has provided us with yet another layer of goodness. He has given us grace.

Grace is a gift. It cannot be earned, and it cannot be bought. It is given freely from an abundantly loving God.

If we measure it in terms of wages, what we have earned is death. But the free gift of God is eternal life through Jesus Christ our Lord.

God won't hold our sins against us; assuming we have repented of them. But the gift He is giving us goes above and beyond even that. It is more than a reprieve from the eternal death sentence.

This is a gift of abundance and life for evermore. How amazing is that!

It is said that mercy is not receiving what we deserve. Grace, on the other hand, is receiving something good, that we certainly don't deserve.

It was our long anticipated, looked forward to date night. We had established this routine some years previously. When our children were all very young, it used to be date night at home, with the children all being put to bed by 7.30.

By this time, our oldest child was old enough to be a babysitter for us, so we had progressed our date nights to going out for an hour or so.

All was going along peacefully, and it all looked on track for us to leave the house at the normal time. Each child was engaged usefully in their various activities.

Then, just as we were about to walk out the door, chaos erupted.

One of our children had been creating a beautiful picture. Great care had been put into this masterpiece, and the child was pardonably pleased with the result. 'My best picture ever' had been the proud description of the drawing. Then, for some reason, an upset happened, and our young child reacted with enormous agitation. In a flash of anger, she picked up her own prized picture and ripped it into little pieces. Then the stormy tears started. 'It was my favourite picture!'

It was obvious that we couldn't walk out the door now with the tempest of frustration and upset that was going on. The problem needed to be dealt with.

My reaction was one of anger and indignation. My child had wilfully destroyed her own work in a moment of bad temper, and then was proceeding to cry noisily about its destruction. 'Why did you do it?' I demanded. I could see the opportunity of date night disappearing, with the more pressing need of dealing with the situation.

My obvious displeasure did nothing to dispel the storm of tears. If anything, they intensified.

Then Robert did something I haven't forgotten.

Quietly, without a word of censure, Robert picked up the pieces of the ripped picture, and began the laborious task of putting them together. It was a bit like doing a jigsaw puzzle. Eventually, he had the picture pieces matching, and then proceeded to tape it together.

The tears and noise gradually subsided, as our child looked on at the loving gesture that was being given. Discipline for the flare of temper was probably what she had been anticipating would happen. And no doubt it would have been the more deserved option.

But instead, her loving father responded to her need for comfort, instead of reprimanding her for the offence that had been committed.

What she needed at that moment was affirmation. She needed to know that, despite the unacceptable tantrum that had been displayed, she was still loved, she was still accepted, and she was forgiven.

Robert chose not to take the pathway of punishment. He chose to offer consolation. Even more, he went beyond that, and took the time-consuming steps to restore the ruined picture.

It cost him: he too had been looking forward to our evening out. He too was disappointed at the lost opportunity. He was also feeling frustrated at the needlessness of the problem.

But he did not demur; he gave his time and energy to serving a greater need.

I realised a moment of truth, and grasped a teachable moment. Looking directly at my tear-stained child, I said: 'This is what grace is about!'

She nodded in comprehension. She could see it too.

What extravagant love God pours out on us! We don't deserve it. In fact, what we really deserve is punishment, because, time and again, we let Him down. Time and again, we give in to the impulses of our flesh, and we act in ways that must disappoint Him terribly – sometimes even in self-destructive ways. But in spite of our ragged behaviour, in spite of our deceitful hearts, He shows us His amazing love through His gift of grace, our Lord Jesus Christ.

> "For God so loved the world that he gave his one and only Son, that whoever believes in him shall not perish but have eternal life. For God did not send his Son into the world to condemn the world, but to save the world through him" (John 3:16,17).

There are a lot of lessons about grace to learn from the story of the sinful woman who came to Jesus and anointed his feet. Her story is found in Luke 7.

Luke tells us that Jesus was invited to a dinner at the home of a Pharisee. During the course of the meal, a woman of the town, who was known for her sinful life, came in with a jar of perfume. She proceeded to weep over Jesus' feet, wipe the tears off with her hair, and to anoint his feet with the perfume. Her actions were bold. She did not let the label of 'sinful woman' define who she was; instead she faced her inadequacies in a brave and life-changing way.

I can imagine how I would have acted if I were in her shoes.

I imagine myself hesitating at the door of the house, struggling with enormous doubts and fears. In my hand is the gift I plan to pour out on Jesus, but fear is stopping me from following through. How would I cope with the condemnation of the people inside the house? Worse still, what if Jesus reacted toward me with loathing, what if he spurned my gift? What if I had taken myself beyond the realm of forgiveness? What if he gave me that look that told me there was no hope for me? What if he told me I had to get my life sorted out before I came to see him? I would know it would be no more than what I deserved, but what a crushing blow such responses would be.

Maybe it would be better just to go away and not risk that rejection. Maybe I should just carry on as I always have ...

Not so with this lady. Despite the fears and doubts that were probably in her mind, she courageously carried on with her plan. She had seen enough of Jesus to feel confident of a gracious response to her gesture. She humbled herself, came before him in her sinful state, and encountered life-changing grace. Those expressive eyes rested on her with love and compassion. His words contained affirmation and forgiveness. He accepted her gift, restored her soul, and sent her on her way with a light heart full of the knowledge of forgiveness and love.

Receiving grace

Have we ever doubted God's grace, and ability to forgive us? Have we ever thought we have gone too far to be forgiven? Have we ever thought that salvation was way too remote for us, because we were not good enough, had not done enough, or didn't know enough? Let us not close our hearts to our Lord because of these doubts. Let us take a leaf from the book of this lady, and humbly open the door of our heart for the Lord to come in. He is already aware of the deceit that is within us, and He desperately wants to be allowed the opportunity to help change our deceitful heart. God's gift of forgiveness and grace has been freely offered.

Our Lord just needs us to come to Him in the state we are now, admitting our need; to open our hearts to Him and seek His help. He won't reject anyone who is willing to come to Him. If only we can believe it. If only we can receive and accept it.

Grace is freely offered to us; but do we sometimes deny ourselves its offer? Do we sometimes say 'No thanks'?

It's a sobering thought!

Thinking that we are not good enough, or have gone too far to be forgiven, is one aspect of denying ourselves grace.

Another aspect of denying ourselves grace is when we don't realise that we even need it. This was certainly the situation with another key player in the sinful woman story. Simon the Pharisee, who had invited Jesus to come and eat with him, had a grace challenged response to the interaction between Jesus and the sinful woman.

Simon's thoughts were along the lines of: 'Doesn't he even realise what a sinful woman this is?' He missed the beautiful connection that was happening between Jesus and the woman. He missed the fact that another child of God was receiving healing through this interaction. He missed the fact that love was extended, love received, and sins were forgiven.

His reaction rejected grace and missed a moment of connecting love.

Jesus' Parable of Two Debtors pinpointed the problem for Simon.

> "Two people owed money to a certain moneylender. One owed him five hundred denarii, and the other fifty. Neither of them had the money to pay him back, so he forgave the debts of both. Now which of them will love him more?" (Luke 7:41,42).

Simon admitted that the one who had the greater debt cancelled would be the one who would love the moneylender more.

Correct! Jesus drives the point home: Whoever is forgiven more will love more.

Like Simon, self-righteousness is another problem we can encounter in receiving grace. We can be oblivious to our own need for grace. Along with that can come a judgemental attitude towards those who are 'less righteous' than ourselves.

Jesus' Parable of the Tax Collector and the Pharisee highlighted this issue of self-righteousness. The story goes that two men went to the temple to pray. The Pharisee looked up to heaven, and prayed to himself about all the great things he had done. The tax collector could not even raise his eyes heavenward, but poured out his sense of inadequacy: "God, have mercy on me, a sinner", he cried.

The prayer of the Pharisee showed that he was oblivious to his own weaknesses. It also showed he allowed free rein to thoughts of comparison and condemnation, as he looked sideways at his neighbour.

How often have we criticised others for their shortcomings, even just in our thoughts? How often have we been blind to our own areas of weakness?

There is another interesting twist to receiving grace. Another parable that Jesus told was of a man who was let off having to repay an absolutely enormous debt. This man realised that the debt was so big that he couldn't possibly pay. He did exactly what we should be doing when we realise our own enormous debt of sin. He asked for mercy.

Mercy was given. Not only was he not going to be required to repay his debt, not only was he granted a reprieve from a jail sentence, but the staggering amount of money he owed was completely wiped out. He was free of the weight of that terrible debt. He had been given a new beginning.

But this is where the story takes a sad twist. The man was happy to accept the gift of forgiveness for himself, but he didn't recognise the full implications of grace. Where grace is given, it needs to be passed on. The actions that followed his reprieve were far from gracious. When he came across another man who owed him a small sum of money, he ruthlessly demanded payment.

Rather than passing on the grace that had been shown to him, he wanted his pound of flesh. His actions showed that he had not really appreciated what had been done for him. It had not changed his life or caused a softening in his heart.

Extending grace

To receive grace fully, we need not only to accept the grace that has been given us, but we also need to act graciously towards our fellow man.

Grace that is received with a humble, thankful heart, will result in a changed life.

The Apostle Paul writes of it like this:

> "I preached that they should repent and turn to God and demonstrate their repentance by their deeds" (Acts 26:20).

One of the ways that repentance will be shown in our lives, is by the way in which we share and offer grace to other people.

Perhaps these 'other people' have let us down in some way. Perhaps they have hurt or upset us. Perhaps their sins or shortcomings are 'worse' than our own. Maybe they 'owe' us in some way. Maybe they appear to be in a more 'ragged state' than what we think we ourselves are. Whatever the perceived debt is, responding with grace is what God is asking of us.

If we find ourselves succumbing to a judgemental critical attitude, we might need to ask ourselves if we are becoming grace challenged.

Let's think back to the sinful woman's story from Luke 7. The great love that she showed to her Lord in the act of anointing his feet, earned her these words from Jesus:

> "Therefore, I tell you, her many sins have been forgiven – as her great love has shown" (Luke 7:47).

This woman would have gone home that night calm and sure that her sins were forgiven. She had a new beginning. She had been given a chance to live a new life. Her brave actions towards Jesus, and her humble awareness of her unworthiness, opened the door to grace. She would have been filled and overflowing with the glow of that forgiveness. I imagine that from here on in, her actions towards other people would be full of the love and grace that she herself had received from Jesus.

Her story is a beautiful grace-filled one.

This aspect of love is totally inspiring. It is a three-step process. First, love and grace have been offered to us by our most gracious God. Then, when we accept grace, we also accept the responsibility that comes with it. The responsibility that grace places on us involves change to our behaviour, and willingness to share and show grace to others.

May we learn to see and appreciate this wonderful gift. May it motivate and inspire us from the inside out.

Grace is an aspect of love. And love never fails.

> "Dear friends, let us love one another, for love comes from God. Everyone who loves has been born of God and knows God ... because God is love. This is how God showed his love among us: He sent his one and only Son into the world that we might live through him ... Dear friends, since God so loved us, we also ought to love one another" (1 John 4:7-9,11).

"Love is patient, love is kind. It does not envy, it does not boast, it is not proud. It does not dishonour others, it is not self seeking, it is not easily angered, it keeps no record of wrongs. Love does not delight in evil, but rejoices with the truth. It always protects, always trusts, always hopes, always perseveres. Love never fails" (1 Corinthians 13:4-8).

In a nutshell:

- God's love shown in His gift of grace is inspirational. Grace is so necessary for our lives.

- Jesus' interaction with the 'sinful woman' shows us that forgiveness is possible for us all.

- Simon's reaction to Jesus' grace-filled response to the sinful woman warns us of the dangers of self-righteousness.

- Grace comes with responsibility: it needs to change us. Grace needs to be shared with others.

- Grace is a key part of God's inspirational love. We need to receive it, appreciate it, and pass it on.

- Love never fails.

Prayer time:

"May the God who gives endurance and encouragement give you the same attitude of mind toward each other that Christ Jesus had."
"May the grace of the Lord Jesus Christ, and the love of God, and the fellowship of the Holy Spirit be with you all" (Romans 15:5; 2 Corinthians 13:14).

Chapter 18

The faith factor

The heart of the matter, I see, is to trust,
To be faithful for God is also a must!
'Lord, courage I need, to allow this to be,
For faith must be active, please help me to see.'

"Do not conform to the pattern of this world, but be transformed by the renewing of your mind. Then you will be able to test and approve what God's will is – his good, pleasing and perfect will" (Romans 12:2).

"For it is by grace you have been saved, through faith – and this is not of yourselves, it is the gift of God – not by works, so that no one can boast. For we are God's handiwork, created in Christ Jesus to do good works, which God prepared in advance for us to do" (Ephesians 2:8-10).

THE butterfly inside the chrysalis is only a few days away from emerging. Its parts are now fully formed, and all the indications point towards its soon arrival.

The chrysalis has continued to darken in colour. We don't have too much longer to wait to see this butterfly in person!

Meanwhile, our spiritual transformation journey is also progressing. There have been some uncomfortable things to contemplate and do. Each step helps bring us closer to what God wants us to become, and who He wants us to be. He wants us to become someone who has a renewed mind and heart.

We are now at the point of going further and deeper in this process. There is another important attribute required for the process of transformation. When we act on this one, we become an undeserving sinner with a new title: counted righteous.

This action is just as hard as letting go of self. If it was a list of rules and actions that we could tick off, that would be much simpler! But instead it's a life-long choice of trust overriding fear, and faith overriding sight.

In this chapter, we will follow the story of one lady who lived out faith over her fear. Her brave actions earned her a worthy mention in the Bible as a lady of faith. Her actions changed her life dramatically: from a Gentile sinner to becoming a child of God, saved by faith.

From what we know of her story in the Bible, maybe the unknown details could have looked something like the dramatisation I have given it in this chapter:

Rumours were rife about spies in the city. Rahab had heard talk about them from many of the townsfolk, and the usual stream of patrons that would normally frequent her home was vastly reduced. Fear was showing plainly on people's faces. Panic was in the hushed tones of urgent conversations that were happening all through the city.

The Israelites were the people responsible for the fear. Their God, it was rumoured, had allowed these people to conquer great kings, and had caused the water of the

Red Sea to dry up. All the towns around mighty Jericho were fearful. Something was definitely afoot.

Rahab had heard of the approach of these people; word had gone ahead about the trail of destruction they were leaving in their wake. Now there were spies here, in her city, with the obvious intent of causing more mischief. It was no wonder the authorities were on edge. Word had gone out for every city dweller to be on the alert for the spies; they needed to be caught!

Not that Jericho should have had anything to fear. They had fine strong walls, that should have been able to withstand any army. But this was no ordinary army; not with a God on their side who could make the water of the sea dry up!

A plan was forming in Rahab's mind. A daring, scary plan, that had the possibility of death for her if it all went wrong. On the other hand, if the Israelites' God came through with another show of His miraculous power, then the whole city was doomed anyway.

She would do it. She would find the spies, and invite them into her home ...

Faith is trust in action. The meaning of the word 'faith' is that of persuasion, or a moral conviction about something. It is to be assured of something, to believe something, even when there may be no concrete proof for it. Faith and trust are so similar that it's difficult to separate the two. They go hand in hand.

Hebrews 11:1 puts it this way:

"Now faith is confidence in what we hope for and assurance about what we do not see."

Faith is about believing something to be true, even when we can't see or touch it.

Rahab's action, spurred on by her conviction and belief in something that she had not yet experienced, is a marvellous example of trust. What she had heard about Israel's God was sufficient for her to take some very bold action, and invite the spies into her home.

Faith in action is important to our transformation process. It is the opposite of gaining righteousness through our own strength.

Works that are done in our own grim determination to be better, do good, live right, and tick the boxes, is doomed to either disappointing failure or prideful self-righteousness.

On the other hand, righteousness that is imputed by God, because of faith, takes the emphasis off what we have done, and places the emphasis on God's gift of grace. Grace is made possible because of Christ's sacrifice. Grace is extended out of the delight that God feels as another child reaches out their hands to Him, and says: 'I believe, please help my unbelief. Please help me ...'

The book of Romans has a lot to say regarding faith and righteousness. Listen to these verses:

"This righteousness is given through faith in Jesus Christ to all who believe" (Romans 3:22).

"For all have sinned and fall short of the glory of God, and all are justified freely by his grace through the redemption that came by Christ Jesus" (verses 23,24).

"What does the Scripture say? 'Abraham believed God, and it was credited to him as righteousness'" (4:3).

"Now to the one who works, wages are not credited as a gift but as an obligation. However, to the one who does not work but trusts God who justifies the ungodly, their faith is credited as righteousness" (verses 4,5).

These verses can almost seem a contradiction to the idea of any form of action on our part. They almost make it sound like all we have to do is sit back, and declare that we believe. However, we are also told that "Faith without works is dead" (James 2:20,26, KJV), so there must be more to it than just curling up in the cosy armchair and declaring that we have faith!

Rahab hurried the men into her house. She had found them, but she also knew that she had been seen. People were used to men entering her house – that was not unusual – but these were not the usual type of men! Time was of the essence; she must hide them. Already there was an insistent banging on her door. With blood pounding in her head, she quickly covered the men with some stalks of flax that were lying on her roof, and ran down the stairs to the door.

Messengers from the king stood outside her door. 'We know some men have come to your house, Rahab, bring them out now, they are spies!'

Willing her voice to be steady, she replied: 'Oh, those men! (Really, are they spies?!) Yes, they did come to my house, but they have gone now. If you leave quickly, you might still catch them.'

She schooled her expression to be one of wide-eyed innocence as she steadily regarded the king's messengers at her door. The soldiers hurried back to the king, with the message that he needed to summon men from the army to go and catch the spies beyond the city gates.

Shaking, but relieved, Rahab went back inside, and made her way up onto the roof. She needed to talk to the men.

"I know that the LORD has given this land to you and that a great fear of you has fallen on us, so that all who live in this country are melting in fear because of you … Everyone's courage failed because of you, for the LORD your God is God in heaven above and on the earth below. Now then, please swear to me by the LORD that you will show kindness to my family, because I have shown kindness to you."

There, it was said. Her fate was now in their hands, and in the hands of their God, in whom she had just expressed her belief and trust.

The men were agreeable to her request, but they too had conditions:

"This oath you made us swear will not be binding on us unless, when we enter the land, you have tied this scarlet cord in the window through which you let us down, and unless you have brought your father, mother, your brothers and all your family into your house. If any of them go outside your house into the street, their blood will be on their own heads; we will not be responsible."

Rahab agreed to their conditions and then hastily sent them on their way, letting them down the wall from the window of her house. It was important for them to go quickly, for the authorities were already combing the surrounding countryside in their desperate search for the men.

Rahab watched them out of sight, and then turned to make preparation for the work she had to do: a scarlet cord in the window, and family informed that they needed to be in her house for when the men came back, otherwise they would not be saved.

Rahab sincerely hoped it would not be a long wait. The thought of being in confined proximity with certain members of her family for a long time was not very appealing!

We see in Rahab's story a faith that is expressed, and a faith that is acted upon. There is expression of belief, and there is action. The two went hand-in-hand. If Rahab had merely expressed belief in Israel's God being all-powerful; saying that she truly believed that He would conquer her land – but had not taken any action to get on side with the spies, and had not boldly asked for their protection, or done what they told her to do – then the outcome of this story would have been very different. Not that God is incapable of saving a person who expresses belief in Him, by any or many other creative means, but Rahab's bold actions meant that her whole family were saved. All because of her faith in action.

Faith in action can take on many different expressions. For Abraham, faith was expressed by God saying, "Go", and Abraham going. Even if it meant giving up all he knew – his comfortable home, his extended family – and going to live a nomadic life of constantly pitching tents.

Faith for Sarah meant 'obeying' her husband, and respecting his wishes for her to be known as his sister, even though it meant uncomfortable consequences happening. Twice.

Faith for Simeon and Anna, in the days leading up to Jesus birth, was expressed by 'waiting'. Both of them were very old, but they were looking for the Messiah, waiting for the indication that 'this' baby was the one. It was said of Simeon that he was waiting for the consolation of Israel, and that he had been told by the Holy Spirit that he would not die before he saw the Lord's Messiah. So he waited, and he watched faithfully.

Anna never left the temple, but worshipped night and day, fasting and praying, also watching faithfully for the Messiah.

Noah expressed his faith by 'doing'. When God told him to build an ark to house not only himself and family, but every type of animal, Noah did so. This was a massive task that took years, and one that, no doubt, opened Noah up to a huge amount of ridicule.

For some, faith is expressed by 'staying'. They choose to stay put rather than run away, because they know that, despite the discomfort they are currently experiencing, it's for a greater good that they stay where they are rather than leave. Hosea's experience was like this. He was not only asked to stay with his adulterous wife, and raise her illegitimate children, but he had to take her back as his wife again, even after she ran away from him.

These people all acted on their faith in a way that showed their trust in God. Their trust was the motivation for them to submit to some very uncomfortable situations!

Belief, faith and trust motivate and move us. Faith gives us a reason to trust. Faith in God gives us Someone to trust in! Faith motivates our actions. It reassures our heart, and gives us direction.

Faith inspires hope.

What might faith in action look like for us?

Here are a few things that are important to all of us, when it comes to active faith:

- Believing that God is.

- Trusting and relying on God despite our fear. This includes believing God, and what is written in His Word. It requires us to believe that God is in control, even in the face of chaos.

- Believing that we are loved, and that there is a future for us.

- Believing that Jesus is the Way, the Truth, and the Life.

- Believing that Jesus really is coming back.

- Believing that God really does want us in His Kingdom.

- Believing that our repented sins have been forgiven.

Faith has us desiring to align ourselves with God's direction, accepting His correction, and trusting His protection. Faith listens, acknowledges and obeys. Faith inspires us to submit to God.

Faith takes us outside of our comfort zone, and extends us in ways that can be decidedly uncomfortable. A life of faith can be a wild but exhilarating ride.

Stepping out in faith grows us immensely. It builds our confidence in God like nothing else will.

God loves us to live a life of active faith. It tells Him that we trust Him, that we believe Him, and that we are prepared to step out of our comfortable lives to live out our convictions. This means so much to Him that He is prepared to consider us as 'righteous' because of this active faith. Not because we deserve it, or have earned it, but because He is so delighted when we show a belief that is filled with active trust.

Rahab was feeling restless. It had been over six days now since the spies had left her house. So far there was no sign of action. The city was still on high alert, but the mood was slightly more relaxed as the week went by. There was no sign of any imminent attack.

The mood inside the house was less than jovial. Spending a week in the close confines of a lot of family members had caused tension. Not only that, but some of her siblings were grumbling, suggesting that maybe nothing was going to happen after all. Rahab's nerves were getting stretched thin; she didn't know how much longer she was going to be able to keep everyone calm. It was hard enough dealing with her own doubts!

She went up to the rooftop again, for the umpteenth time, to scan the horizon. The scarlet cord hung limply from the window, taunting her decision to throw her lot in with Israel and their God. Surely they would come!

Finally, something was happening. Rahab had almost lost count of the days they had been waiting. But now she could see signs of activity. The Israelite army was on the move.

Fear and excitement coursed through her. Finally, the Israelites were going to attack. What would they do, she wondered? What amazing strategy would they employ?

Unbelievable. They were doing nothing but walking around the city, blowing trumpets! Six days, so far, of walking round the wall. How was this going to work? How was walking around a wall going to do any damage? The headache that had been pounding in Rahab's head for the last week was becoming intense. If one more person were to ask her what the Israelites were up to, she felt she would snap ...!

But this seventh day the Israelites had charged it up a bit. Rather than just once around the wall, they were clocking up the miles. Seven times round.

The whole family were on the roof watching. There was a feeling of nervous excitement among everyone now. They could all feel that something big was about to happen. There was an air of confidence in the demeanour of the Israelites. Victory was going to be theirs.

The many days of waiting, watching, and believing against the odds were about to be rewarded for Rahab and her family.

Faith plays an important part when it comes to transformational change. Faith and trust are the fuel behind the renewing of the mind that is needed. Colossians 3 gives us a whole list of things that we need to put to 'death' from our earthly nature: sexual immorality, impurity, lust, evil desires, greed, anger, rage, malice, slander, filthy language, lying.

Galatians 5:19-21 lists a few more:

"The acts of the flesh are obvious: sexual immorality, impurity and debauchery; idolatry and witchcraft; hatred, discord, jealousy, fits of rage, selfish ambition, dissensions, faction and envy; drunkenness, orgies, and the like ..."

These things are our default setting; they are the natural state of the deceitful heart. They might seem comfortable, natural. Some of them are even things that we feel we have a right to have, or to engage in.

It's going to take knowledge that is based on God being trustworthy, and action based on faith, to become the driving force behind our willingness to let go of those things that come so naturally.

We need a faith that believes that God has our best interests in mind. This faith accepts that whatever He is asking us to get rid of, must be because He has something better in mind for us.

The things from our earthly nature shackle us to death. They are dead weights, and stop us from living out our potential. They inhibit the Spirit fruit which God wants us to be producing.

An active faith enables us to feed the desire to be aligned with God's Spirit, rather than to be conformed to the pattern of this world. Faith renews our mind.

Faith like this allows God to access the deepest, darkest parts of our heart. It agrees to God using the 'knife' that can scrape out the muck that's there: the defensiveness, self-justification and denial. It helps us acknowledge our weakness, and confess our sins. It allows God to open our eyes to the truth about ourselves. It helps us make daily choices to sacrifice our way in favour of His way.

Let us pray for this sort of faith. Let us ask God to help us Know, Believe and Trust. Let us ask God to help us let go of all that hinders our growth, and all that binds us to our earthly nature.

This was the faith that motivated Rahab to her actions. She spurned the natural reliance on the strength of the city walls that her countrymen were relying on. Instead, she chose to throw off the life she had always known, and throw in her lot with a strange group of people and their God.

Faith inspired her. Faith drove her actions.

This is the way of faith.

Rahab looked down at the tiny infant in her arms. He was so perfect, so beautiful! She looked from her tiny son to her strong, courageous husband. Her past life was but a distant memory. How long ago that seemed! That past life held no desire for her now. No longer did she want to lie in the arms of many different men. No longer did she want to live in idolatry. No longer did she want the ways and immoral practices of her former countrymen. That life was all gone, and she did not miss it.

She reflected instead on how blessed she felt to be married to this wonderful man, and to have borne him this gorgeous baby boy. She could not fathom how anyone would have wanted to marry her: a prostitute, and a foreigner. But it had happened. Now she was married, and had a child. What amazed her still further was that she had been adopted and accepted into the large family of God's people. What an Awesome God these people had! And this God was now her God.

Tears ran silently down her cheeks, as she felt overcome all over again by the amazing grace that had been bestowed on her.

Her lips formed the words she had spoken many times since she had left Jericho: 'Thank you, my Lord!'

"In the same way, was not even Rahab the prostitute considered righteous for what she did when she gave lodging to the spies and sent them off in a different direction?" (James 2:25)

May we also desire to grow a faith that will help us let go of anything that might inhibit transformation. May we aspire towards action inspired by trust in God. May we, like Rahab, be considered righteous because of our faith in action.

In a nutshell:

- The works that come from our own strength cannot save us.

- Faith imputes righteousness; not on our own merits, but by God's generous gift of grace, through the sacrifice and work of Jesus.

- Faith is belief and trust in action.

- Faithful action is based not so much on our own inclinations, but on God's direction.

- Living by faith can be uncomfortable, but it's also life changing.

- Faith becomes the motivation behind our willingness to remove, or take off the ways of the flesh from our lives.

- Stepping out in faith grows us, and builds our confidence in God like nothing else.

Prayer time:

Pray that God might open your eyes to His direction today. Pray that He will give you the strength and courage to act on that direction, the humility to receive His correction, and a thankful heart for His protection. Pray that your faith may be alive and active!

Chapter 19

The teacup process

'There's another thing, child', I hear the Lord say,
'Times will come in your life when I strip things away,
A furnace of fire, it may feel it can be,
It's called refining, you see, to help draw you to me.'

'Take a teacup, for instance, to help you compare,
Its beauty is made with design and great care,
But once it was just a great lump of dry clay,
Until it was moulded and shaped in this way.'

'You too, like this cup, need some shaping to grow,
It may feel like it hurts, but I want you to know,
I really do know just what I am doing,
The process takes time, but your heart is renewing!'

"Yet you, LORD, are our Father. We are the clay, you are the potter; we are the work of your hand" (Isaiah 64:8).

"Therefore, since we have been justified through faith, we have peace with God through our Lord Jesus Christ, through whom we have gained access by faith into this grace in which we now stand. And we boast in the hope of the glory of God. Not only so, but we also glory in our sufferings, because we

know that suffering produces perseverance; perseverance,
character; and character, hope. And hope does not put us
to shame, because God's love has been poured out into our
hearts ..." (Romans 5:1-5).

A N older couple, who frequently visited antique shops, had a love for pottery, especially teacups.

One day they came across a particularly fine and beautiful teacup. As they examined it more closely, the teacup suddenly spoke.

'You know, I haven't always been a tea cup. There was a time when I was just a lump of clay. My master took me and rolled me, and patted me all over; he pummelled and pushed me about. I yelled out, "Leave me alone", but he only smiled and said, "Not yet." I was spun round and round, until I was dizzy. "Stop it", I screamed. But the master only nodded, and said, "Not yet."

'Then he put me in the oven. It felt so hot. I yelled, and knocked on the door. I could read his lips as he shook his head, "Not yet."

'Finally he took me out, and put me on a shelf to cool down. I felt so relieved. But then he brushed me and painted me all over. The fumes made me gag! "Stop it", I cried. He only nodded, "Not yet."

'He put me into another oven. This one was even hotter than the first. I begged and pleaded. He smiled sympathetically, and said, "Not yet."

'When I had given up hope of ever getting out of that oven, he finally opened the door, and took me out, and placed me on a shelf to cool down. One hour later, he brought me a mirror, and said, "Look at yourself." I looked in disbelief at the reflection. "That's not me, it couldn't be me, it's beautiful!"

'"I want you to remember", the master said, "I know it hurt to be rolled and patted, but if I had just left you, you'd have dried up. I know it made you dizzy to spin round on the wheel, but if I had stopped, you would have crumbled. I know it hurt and it was hot and disagreeable in the oven, but if I hadn't put you there, you would have cracked. I know the fumes were bad when I brushed and painted you all over, but if I hadn't done that, you never would have hardened. Without the paint, you would not have had any colour in your life, and if I hadn't put you back in that second oven, you wouldn't have survived for very long because the hardness would not have held. Now you are a finished product. You are what I had in mind when I first began with you."'

Character building

I said in the previous chapter that there is nothing that helps us grow quite like stepping out in faith. It is true, but there is more. Stepping out in faith grows our confidence enormously, and changes us radically. But God frequently uses another method to grow us as well: Testing. This is designed to help us grow character, and to learn more about trust. Depending on our reaction to each situation, it will do just that.

- When our ordered life seems to have gone to custard ...
- When there has been a curveball thrown into the mix ...
- When things are feeling uncomfortable ...
- When there seems to be no answer ...
- When circumstances are pressing in hard ...
- When we feel pushed, pulled and pummelled ...
- When everything we have previously relied on has been stripped away ...

These are the times when our trust in God is tested and tried. These are the moments when we either hold on tightly to faith, or we let it go.

Through these trials, God is refining, shaping, and growing our character, in a similar way to the master potter with the lump of clay. The master potter is creating a beautiful teacup; God is creating a beautiful transformed person.

Our challenge is to keep holding on. He's not finished with us yet.

The book of James has a lot to say on the subject of testing:

"Consider it pure joy, my brothers and sisters, whenever you face trials of many kinds, because you know that the testing of your faith produces perseverance. Let perseverance finish its work so that you may be mature and complete, not lacking anything" (James 1:2-4).

"As you know, we count as blessed those who have persevered. You have heard of Job's perseverance and have seen what the Lord finally brought about. The Lord is full of compassion and mercy" (5:11).

Often, when we take our first small tentative step of faith, God will stretch us and push us to another level. He wants our faith to grow and expand. Sometimes this happens through the unexpected curveballs of life.

The story of the Widow of Zarephath illustrates this.

It was drought time. Water and food were very scarce. The brook Elijah was drinking from had dried up, and he needed to find some other source of water and food. God sent Elijah to a poor widow woman in Zarephath. Elijah came across her collecting wood to make a fire on which she was going to cook the last of her food, for herself and her son.

Faith test number one: Elijah asked her if she could bring him a drink. Remember, it is drought time, and water was scarce. Water supplies were drying up everywhere, just like Elijah's brook. However, the lady did not demur, and turned to go into the house to bring Elijah a drink.

Faith test number two: Elijah asked her to bring him some food as well. This time she made a protest. "As the LORD your

God lives", she says, "I don't have any bread – only a handful of flour in a jar, and a little olive oil in a jug. I am gathering a few sticks to take home and make a meal for myself and my son, that we may eat it – and die." Nevertheless, Elijah persisted with his request, promising that if she did as he asked, her food wouldn't run out. The woman complied, and rose to the challenge. She took her first tentative step of faith.

Elijah's promise held firm. The flour and oil never ran out the whole time Elijah stayed with the widow.

Imagine how her faith would have grown through this incident. With a feeling of renewed wonder, she would come to her jar every morning, to discover that once again there was enough in it for that day. And the next. And the next.

Faith test number three: Some time later, the woman's son became ill, and he died. In great distress, the woman turned to Elijah, and pinned responsibility on him. "What do you have against me, man of God? Did you come to remind me of my sin and kill my son?"

Elijah took the boy's body, and in turn cried out to God. "LORD my God, have you brought tragedy even on this widow I am staying with, by causing her son to die?"

This test of faith was not only for the widow, but also for Elijah. There is deep disappointment and despair attached to this story. Surely a good deed, and such steps of faith, could not be so rewarded? Why has God allowed such a story of faith to end with bitterness and sorrow? This is not the ending we would expect for faithful obedience.

But God has more growth in mind for the faith that has already been expressed by the poor widow woman.

Elijah stretched himself upon the boy three times, and cried out to God for the boy's life to be returned to him.

Elijah's faith was rewarded, and the boy's life returned. Elijah took the boy and gave him back to his mother. "Look, your son is alive!"

Maybe the miracles of the never-ending flour and oil supply had not been enough. Maybe she needed further confirmation of God's power and Elijah's authenticity. Listen to the woman's response:

> "Now I know that you are a man of God and that the word of the LORD from your mouth is the truth."

God, in His wisdom, did not leave this woman with only a jar full of faith. Her story was set to end with a whole heart full of faith and belief!

What, more than why

A while ago, I heard this thought expressed: 'In the tough times of life, we should not so much ask "why", as "what".'

- What could I be learning from this situation?
- What is God trying to teach me?
- What is God trying to do with me?
- What can I do about this situation?
- What is my reaction going to be?
- In what way am I growing?

Quite a while ago, when our children were all still in primary school, I experienced God stripping from my life some of the things I relied on.

I had been feeling very comfortable with my life. I had a good group of school mums with whom I enjoyed catching up every day after school when I went to pick up my children. My children also had some good friendships with the children of these families. We spent time in each other's homes with various social activities. Life was feeling good and comfortable.

Then, one by one, these families all started leaving the school. Some shifted out of the area altogether. Others decided to shift their children to different schools. This all happened over the course of a year.

As they all left, I felt very bereft of the friendships that I had built up over the course of time my children had been at that school. Not only that, but my children also were feeling the effects of losing some close friendships. It felt like our comfort zone had been invaded, and we were left feeling alone and empty. I recall feeling quite miserable. So were my children!

Then one day, I recalled a prayer I had been somewhat casually praying just a short time before: 'Lord please help my faith to grow ... Increase my faith ...'

It gradually occurred to me that God was answering that prayer; but not in any way that I would have anticipated. He was beginning the process by stripping away the things I had been relying on. I had been basing my assurance on the happiness and comfort of having friends around me. I had been lulled into a false sense of security by relying too heavily on having these people around. My sense of security, I came to realise, was not based so much on God (who is a Rock, and who never moves), but rather on the transient and shifting sand of other people. I was relying very heavily on people support and friendship, and spending too little time building a relationship with God, and relying on Him.

So God started to stretch my faith by stripping away the reliance I was placing on other people rather than Him.

Through this experience, I found that life did not fall completely apart when my friends left. Over time, God supplied other friendships. More importantly, I was learning I should turn to God for my sense of security more than I should look for it in other people.

God was keenly interested in growing a faith in me based on my reliance on Him, rather than the other props in my life that I had been leaning on.

Holding on to hope

Romans 5:3-5 tells us that suffering produces perseverance, and perseverance produces character, and character produces hope.

Hope is a crucial element to holding on to our faith. Without hope, we are hopeless.

The people who best survive the most horrible situations are those who hold on to some form of hope. Those who give up on hope, give up trying.

How blessed we are, as believers, to have an amazing hope! We have hope in knowing that we have a God who loves us, and who has our best interests at heart. We have hope in forgiveness. We have hope in resurrection, which is shown emphatically in the fact that Jesus was raised; his resurrection is the guarantee of our resurrection being a reality. We have hope in God's grace being extended to us; not because we deserve it, but because of His enormous love, shown through the death and resurrection of our Lord Jesus.

Some time ago I asked for stories from people that show how they have seen God working in their lives through tough times. One lady wrote of the pain of losing a loved son when he was only in his forties. Another wrote of having struggled for years with financial stress when her husband was unable to work. Yet another wrote of the stress endured at the time that her young son suffered a car accident that nearly robbed him of his life. Another young lady wrote of the struggles that she has had both mentally and physically all her life.

Expressions of hope and trust were prominent features of all these stories. Each of them held on to the hope that there was a brighter future ahead. They expressed trust that God is in control, no matter how hard or out of control their situation seemed to be.

I love the message of hope and trust penned by this young lady. She has struggled with mental health issues for many years:

'I have learnt that I need to rely on God like I rely on others to look after me. Even though life is difficult, God has looked after me, and I am thankful for His guidance in my life that helps me not to quit my faith in Him. The straight and narrow path leads to the kingdom. I am looking forward to the kingdom and I wouldn't have learnt lots if I hadn't gone through the things that I have. God has a plan for each one of us. Please don't give up on your journey to the kingdom.'

We frequently see beautiful things emerge from hard, hot or irritating circumstances. Gold is purified through heat. A pearl is created by irritation from sand. A diamond is formed through pressure. A teacup needs pummelling, shaping and heat to become what it's meant to be. The wings of a butterfly need fluid pumped into them to make them work; the struggle to emerge from a chrysalis helps aid this process.

So it is with us. God wants us to grow. He wants to build character, perseverance, resilience and hope. He wants us to build trust in Him. He does this by stretching our faith, and putting us outside our comfort zones. Like a parent tries to encourage a child to try something new, so God allows situations in our lives that will help us to grow and trust in Him.

The Psalmist in Psalm 119 recognised the immense benefit that affliction brought him:

"Before I was afflicted I went astray, but now I obey your word ... It was good for me to be afflicted so that I might learn your decrees" (Psalm 119:67,71).

Talk about transformation! This man had an obedience about-turn, all because of the tough times in his life.

If only the stretching and testing in our lives might bear similar fruit. If only we can hold on, and hang in there.

One day, an exquisite 'teacup' will be revealed. One day the trials of the tough times will bear fruit in a beautiful transformed character.

The butterfly that will have emerged in its struggle from the chrysalis, will eventually open its lovely strong wings and fly.

Let us hold on with hope and anticipation for that bright and wonderful day, when our transformation will be complete.

Just as we conclude this chapter, come with me for one final visit to the chrysalis hanging from its leaf.

It is now completely transparent. The vibrant colours and pattern of the butterfly inside can be seen very clearly.

This is all indication that the butterfly is ready to emerge. This will be the day for it to begin its new transformed life.

In a nutshell:

- God stretches and grows our faith through trials and uncomfortable circumstances in life. He wants us to grow in character, perseverance and hope.

- We can help facilitate that growth, and learn to see purpose in it, by asking the 'what' questions, rather than 'why'.

- We need to hold on tightly to hope. Hope will see us through the tough times, and help us see beyond the here and now, to the bright future ahead.

Prayer time:

'Dear Lord, thank you for your love. Please help us to see your love in all the situations of our lives. Please help us to see your purpose in the tough times, to hold on to hope, and to allow you to grow perseverance and character within us. Please help us to grow to be more like your Son. Amen.'

Chapter 20

Spirit fruit

"So I say, walk by the Spirit, and you will not gratify the desires of the flesh. For the flesh desires what is contrary to the Spirit, and the Spirit what is contrary to the flesh. They are in conflict with each other, so that you are not to do whatever you want. But if you are led by the Spirit, you are not under the law" (Galatians 5:16-18).

"No good tree bears bad fruit, nor does a bad tree bear good fruit. Each tree is recognised by its own fruit. People do not pick figs from thornbushes, or grapes from briers. The good man brings good things out of the good stored up in his heart, and the evil man brings evil things out of the evil stored up in his heart. For the mouth speaks what the heart is full of" (Luke 6:43-45).

"Do not be deceived: God cannot be mocked. A man reaps what he sows. Whoever sows to please their flesh, from the flesh will reap destruction; whoever sows to please the Spirit, from the Spirit will reap eternal life" (Galatians 6:7,8).

"Since we live by the Spirit, let us keep in step with the Spirit" (5:25).

THE chrysalis case was empty.

It hung limply from its leaf, transparent in the sunlight. There was a hole in one end of it where something had recently emerged.

The previous day it had been full, swollen with the life that was within. It had looked like something that was pregnant and ready to give birth. The markings and colour of the butterfly inside had been discernible. The signs had all indicated that the butterfly was ready to emerge.

Today it was empty. The life within had been released, and the chrysalis case was an unneeded item. It had served its purpose.

Have we ever looked at an empty chrysalis case and thought that it was a useless, pathetic thing hanging there in its emptiness? Have we ever felt saddened that it was no longer needed?

Probably not. More likely, we would look briefly at the empty chrysalis case, and then turn to look around for a sighting of the butterfly that had obviously come out. The chrysalis case would hang there as a memento of triumph. Although it no longer contained life, it had nonetheless been an essential part of the awe-inspiring transformation.

The empty chrysalis was a sign that successful change had happened.

So, what about us? Where are we now on our transformation journey? How is the process of becoming empty to self going? Are we beginning to see that diminishing in the way of self, or flesh, actually enlarges us? Are we beginning to see that being empty of self, the way of the flesh, is actually a triumph?

Because it is only by becoming empty to ourselves that a 'butterfly' can be revealed. It is only by becoming empty to ourselves that we can say 'yes' to the way of the Spirit.

The Spirit and the flesh are at variance with each other.

"For the flesh desires what is contrary to the Spirit, and the Spirit what is contrary to the flesh."

We don't have an empty chrysalis case to give any outward sign of successful transformation, but according to God's Word, there are some outward markers that indicate that transformation is occurring in our lives.

It's described as fruit in the Bible. Fruit of God's Spirit.

"Each tree is recognised by its own fruit ..." (Luke 6:44).

Here is what Spirit fruit looks like:

"But the fruit of the Spirit is love, joy, peace, forbearance, kindness, goodness, faithfulness, gentleness and self-control. Against such things there is no law. Those who belong to Christ Jesus have crucified the flesh with its passions and desires. Since we live by the Spirit, let us keep in step with the Spirit" (Galatians 5:22-25).

I don't know about you, but this is not something that I can achieve in my own strength! I try, but way too frequently, I fail. More often than not, I react with impatience, rather than patience. My mind often feels more like chaos than peace. The smile of joy gets a bit wobbly at times. Self-control ...? Too often lacking! Love ...? Well, sort of, on my terms ...

We need help to achieve any of this. Victory will not be in our strength, but in His!

Without a doubt, God wants us to succeed. And He has given us ways, strategies and disciplines that can help us along the way. We have already seen how faith helps us let go of the rotten fruit of the flesh. We have seen how God is pruning us through trials and difficulties, so that we can produce the right fruit.

Now, with further help – and a deep desire on our part – we will journey on towards "living by the Spirit", and "keeping in step with the Spirit".

God has equipped us for this journey by giving us some good disciplines to practice. He has told us what the good fruit looks like. He has told us what to think about, and what to 'clothe' ourselves with, so that we can produce the right kind of fruit.

Thought fruit

"The weapons we fight with are not the weapons of the world. On the contrary, they have divine power to demolish strongholds. We demolish arguments and every pretension that sets itself up against the knowledge of God, and we take captive every thought and make it obedient to Christ" (2 Corinthians 10:4,5).

"Do not conform to the pattern of this world, but be transformed by the renewing of your mind. Then you will be able to test and approve what God's will is – his good, pleasing and perfect will" (Romans 12:2)

Here are some of the thought-filled tools we need in order to develop a transformed mind. Because what we think about is what we become.

The mind is the gateway to walking in step with the Spirit. 'The way a man thinks, so he is.'

Philippians 4:8 tells us how to channel our thoughts, and what to think about:

"Finally brothers and sisters, whatever is true whatever is noble, whatever is right, whatever is pure, whatever is lovely, whatever is admirable – if anything is excellent or praiseworthy – think about these things."

A while ago, I experienced a time when I needed actively to channel my thoughts in the way Paul describes in Philippians. I had been through a very upsetting relationship breakdown. A series of unfortunate circumstances had caused a close friendship to undergo a painful rift. I had gone through a number of emotions, starting with sadness and self-blame. That was followed in short succession by indignation, and a tendency to think about all the shortcomings of the other person involved. These negative thoughts would start to become like a compact disc on replay in my mind as I rehashed every bit of the sorry affair, dwelling on my friend's unforgiving attitude.

Realising that this was a quick road to bitterness, I had to call this verse from Philippians to mind every time I reverted to negative thoughts. I had to make my thought processes go through the Philippians 4:8 test. Is this thought true? Well maybe, at least in part. Is it noble, right, pure, lovely or admirable? No!

I would then instead try to turn my mind to prayer for my friend, to counteract my pitiful and stinking thinking.

In time, our relationship was restored, and the hurt forgiven. But it would have been a very different outcome had I allowed my thoughts to remain in that negative cycle!

To walk in step with the Spirit, we need to have thoughts that are channelled in a healthy and godly way.

Putting on

"But now you must rid yourselves of all such things as these: anger, rage, malice, slander, and filthy language from your lips. Do not lie to each other, since you have taken off your old self with its practices, and have put on the new self, which is being renewed in knowledge in the image of its Creator" (Colossians 3:8-10).

Now that our thoughts have been given a new direction, our words and actions are to get a helping hand. Walking in step with the Spirit requires not only taking off our old self, but putting on something new.

For all those clothes lovers out there, here's our new exciting wardrobe:

"Therefore, as God's chosen people, holy and dearly loved, clothe yourselves with compassion, kindness, humility, gentleness and patience. Bear with each other and forgive one another if any of you has a grievance against someone. Forgive as the Lord forgave you. And over all these virtues put on love, which binds them all together in perfect unity" (verses 12-14).

Jesus' story of the Samaritan and the wounded man illustrates all the above virtues in practice.

Although we are not told, we are going to suppose, for this example, that the wounded man was a Jew.

Mr Samaritan (a natural enemy of any Jew) came across the wounded man, barely alive, lying on the side of the road. He looked on the plight of the wounded man with great compassion. Whatever grievances he might have historically held against his Jewish neighbours were put to the background as he kindly reached out to meet this man's need. With great patience, he bandaged the wounds, and gently supported the man onto his own donkey so he could take him to a place where he could have some ongoing care. With thoughtful love, he went above and beyond his call to duty, and promised to pay whatever costs might be incurred for the man's care.

The Samaritan put off racial discrimination, grudges, discord, jealousy, indignation and hatred, and chose instead to put on compassion, kindness, gentleness, patience and love.

Forgiveness for any racial discrimination that might have come his way previously, was clearly shown in his loving actions.

Compassion inspired him to stop and help. Kindness motivated him to do all he could – and more – for the plight of this man. Loving actions helped him overlook any racial grievances he might have had. Ultimately, out of his compassionate love, he paid the steep price for the man's healing.

Jesus' parable is really his own story. He is our 'Mr Samaritan'. His love for us in our brokenness has gone above and beyond what might humanly be expected. What he has done for us, and shown to us, is the attitude and character that he wants us to put on and show to others. He wants us to be his hands, heart and feet of love.

It's not easy, and it's not cheap. Living a life of love can be costly in many ways!

Some time ago, we had a knock on our door in the mid-evening. Standing in the dark outside our door was a dishevelled and clearly agitated man. He told us he was on the run from the police, but now wanted to hand himself in. He asked us to phone the police to come and get him; he was tired of running.

We were not used to having 'criminals' knocking on our door, asking us to call the police to come and get them, so we felt a little wary of the man.

He told us that he had a car outside, and would wait in his car for the police to arrive.

We phoned the police, as he requested. With a young family at the time, we were hesitant to have the man come into our house, not knowing what sort of mental state he was in, or how safe he was.

One of our young daughters confronted us, her eyes flashing. 'Why are you leaving him to wait outside in his car?' she demanded.

We explained that, as there were young children in the house, we didn't want to expose them to any danger by inviting in this potentially volatile stranger who was on the run from the police. We told her that we would make a cup of coffee for him while he waited.

Going to the cupboard, she chose a mug that had been given as a Sunday School gift some time previously. Written on the side of the mug was 'WWJD?' What would Jesus do?

She personally made the coffee and took it outside to the man. (Robert was already outside with him, helping talk him into a calmer state, while they waited for the police to arrive.)

Given our responsibilities, we had made the decision not to have the man come into our house. Were we acting out of wise parental concern, or were we were also reacting out of fear? Whatever way, we did not go the extra mile. Our young daughter could clearly see that we had not done as much as we could have. The words written on the cup that she chose were ringing in her mind. It was a message she wanted to challenge us with. 'What would Jesus do?' In her mind, she had no doubt: Jesus would have invited the man inside the house!

So often we count the cost, and settle for second best. For all sorts of very logical reasons, it is sometimes too high a cost to give the best.

In our case, we took some of the actions of our Colossians 3 verse, but we didn't go the whole way. In this scenario, we didn't pass the Samaritan love test.

How thankful we can be, however, that Jesus never settled for second best. He went the full way in his show of love. What amazing love he had!

What are some ways we can go about putting on the 'clothing' of love?

We are going to need to ask for Help! As I've already discovered, trying to show love out of just the goodness of my own heart, has very poor and limiting results!

The Lord of love is waiting for our call. We will need to ask Him to open our hearts and minds to receiving His love before we can do anything else. He loved us first. We will need to experience this love first-hand for ourselves.

We will also need to know what it is to be that wounded man lying on the road. As we picture ourselves in his place, we can ask God to open our minds to what our own wounds and brokenness look like. What is it that has us lying there helpless and needy? The wounded man couldn't do anything for himself, except cry out for help. The help he received was radically going to change his life forever. He would never be the same again. No longer would he be able to look on his fellow man with discrimination. No longer would he be able to walk past someone else in need without reaching out a hand. The love shown to him would have washed over him like a refreshing shower. Out of intense and overwhelming gratitude, he too would be on the lookout for ways to show love to others, from that time on.

Recognising our own brokenness and weakness is the starting point for showing God's love in our lives. From there, we can learn to see where the Lord of love is reaching into our lives with His healing touch. We can see how He is showering us with His love. The more love we can see and recognise as coming from Him, the more we will be enabled to have that love flow out from ourselves.

The new wardrobe of compassion, kindness, humility, gentleness, patience, forgiveness and love will be an outward sign of the inward transformation that has been going on. The inward transformation is activated by perceiving and receiving the grace that our Lord has poured out on us.

Armour

To protect our new 'clothes' of compassion, kindness, humility, gentleness, patience, forgiveness and love, God has also supplied us with some other helpful 'armour'. When we put it on, it will help us immensely in our transformation process.

Ephesians 6 describes the armour:

"Therefore put on the full armour of God, so that when the day of evil comes, you may be able to stand your ground, and after you have done everything, to stand. Stand firm then, with the belt of truth buckled around your waist, with the breastplate of righteousness in place, and with your feet fitted with the readiness that comes from the gospel of peace. In addition to all this, take up the shield of faith, with which you can extinguish all the flaming arrows of the evil one. Take the helmet of salvation and the sword of the Spirit, which is the word of God. And pray in the Spirit on all occasions with all kinds of prayers and requests" (Ephesians 6:13-18).

The spiritual equipment of this armour consists of truth, righteousness, the gospel of peace, faith, salvation, the word of God, and prayer.

Most of this equipment is for defence. But the Word of God is described as the sword of the Spirit, which is a weapon of offence. It's to be used to cut and thrust against the evils of the way of the flesh.

Jesus used the sword of the Spirit very tactfully in his battle with temptation in the wilderness. Whatever temptation was thrust before him, he had an answer from the Word. He cut the ground out from under the temptation by his ready knowledge and use of Scripture.

We really do need to have a mind full of scriptural principles and wisdom to use this weapon effectively. To walk in step with the Spirit, we need to use the Spirit's sword that's been provided for us.

God has shown us what tools are necessary to stand against evil. We now need to use the 'armour' that has been provided!

Additions

But wait, there's more! 2 Peter 1:3-9 gives us some helpful steps to use in growing our Spirit fruit muscles:

"His divine power has given us everything we need for a godly life through our knowledge of him who called us by his own glory and goodness" (verse 3).

"For this very reason, make every effort to add to your faith goodness; and to goodness, knowledge; and to knowledge, self-control; and to self-control, perseverance; and to perseverance, godliness; and to godliness, mutual affection; and to mutual affection, love. For if you possess these qualities in increasing measure, they will keep you from being ineffective and unproductive in your knowledge of our Lord Jesus Christ" (verses 5-8).

Peter's advice creates step by step growth in us if we follow it. Each step gives us manageable progress markers to work towards. It could seem overwhelming if we try and do them all at once, so Peter has presented them as ongoing additions. 'Keep growing', he's telling us, 'and here's what you should plant next.' The key is to build these qualities in increasing measure.

To walk in step with the Spirit, we need to keep growing!

The joy factor

"Let us throw off everything that hinders and the sin that so easily entangles. And let us run with perseverance the race marked out for us, fixing our eyes on Jesus, the pioneer and perfecter of faith. For the joy that was set before him he endured the cross, scorning its shame, and sat down at the right hand of the throne of God" (Hebrews 12:1,2).

Remember joy from the first Section of the book? We're back there again. If there is anything that can make the tough things palatable, it's joy. If there is anything that becomes the wind beneath our wings, and allows us to soar above the mire of mediocrity, it's joy.

Focusing on joy, and being full of joy, gave our Lord Jesus the ability to scorn the pleasures of sin for its season. Focusing on joy gave him the strength to endure the pain and shame. Focusing on joy gave Jesus the motivation to go through with his ultimate act of love and selfless giving. Focusing on joy gave his life meaning and purpose. Focusing on joy gave our Lord the ultimate victory.

Joy is a lifesaver. Without joy, we are merely going through the motions. Without joy we spend our days feeling like we 'should' be doing more and being better. We can become consumed with guilt and fear, because we feel like we will never be good enough. Without joy, transformation and living the Christ-life becomes a burden that we have to grit our teeth and bear.

Joy gives colour, motivation and meaning to our actions. Joy infuses us with warmth and hope.

Joy gives us our smile and our inner sparkle. Expressing joy makes others wonder what we've got, and what our secret is! Joy helps make the transformation process beautiful.

Joy makes walking in step with the Spirit enjoyable. Joy is part of the Spirit fruit package.

Let's keep reminding ourselves what there is to be joyful about in our lives. Practise joy daily to receive the most benefit. Joy is beautiful.

It is meant for us to share and show.

By their fruit you will know them

Spirit fruit is one of those outward markers that indicates we are transforming internally. It shows that something beautiful is changing and growing within.

Does that mean we have to show the Fruit of the Spirit perfectly in our lives? What happens when we stuff up? We might have all the right intentions, but then find that we have once again given in to anger and frustration. Or committed 'That' sin again.

I don't know how many times I have been grumpy rather than patient. Or omitted to meet a need and be helpful. Or opened my mouth and spoken sharp words instead of gracious words. Or engaged in unhelpful talk about other people.

No, if I were to mark my transformation progress by having achieved perfection in good fruit, I would have to score a miserable fail!

It could be easy for us to become disheartened at the imperfection of our fruit. We are often looking for instant results, but change is not always instantaneous. It takes time. However, we can be encouraged that we are on the right track, if we can detect in ourselves a desire for God's ways; even if that desire is accompanied by action that is imperfect. Desire shows that we want to walk in harmony with the Spirit. Imperfect action shows that we are willing to try. Each time we try to bend our wayward will to God's way, we change a little bit inside. Maybe the next time we find ourselves in a similar situation to the one that we previously messed up, we might find that we have a little more resilience to react in a different way.

The other factor we should be looking for, and desiring to cultivate, is the fruit of repentance. This shows that we are open to seeing where we are off track, and humble enough to receive correction in that area. Repentance is a fruit that really shows we desire to align ourselves with God, and with His ways.

Acknowledgement, repentance, forgiveness, grace. All of these are fruit that show the way we are becoming empty to self.

Perfecting the art of walking in step with the Spirit is not going to be achieved from our own strength. Our growth is going to come from trying, perhaps failing, repenting, asking for help and being willing to try again. The final triumph will belong to God. Whenever we succeed in a previously difficult area, it will be with all thanks to the power and help that God has given us. We overcome in His strength, not ours.

Proverbs 21:31 puts it this way:

"The horse is made ready for the day of battle, but victory rests with the LORD."

This tells me that my job is to get the 'horse' ready by aligning myself with the Spirit, and to put myself in the best 'battle' position. But the ultimate success of the battle lies with God. It will be His victory.

We can't expect any form of victory, however, if we don't do our part!

Our horse is made ready for the sin battle by being diligent about our thoughts, putting on the right clothes, and using the armour God has provided.

Another story from Corrie Ten Boom's life illustrates this really well.

After her release from the concentration camp, Corrie spent a lot of time travelling around, speaking publicly about God's love and forgiveness.

After one such event she was approached by a man. She recognised him instantly, and felt herself completely freeze up. He was one of the guards from the Ravensbruck prison camp. All the memories came rushing back: his vicious behaviour towards all the women prisoners, the humiliation he caused them to feel, his mocking and callousness. She remembered the suffering all the prisoners had endured. Suffering which had resulted in her sister Betsie's death.

This man was now holding his hand out to her. He told her that she had preached a powerful message that day on forgiveness. He told her that, since those days of the prison camp, he himself was now a Christian. He then asked her if she would forgive him.

She saw the outstretched hand, and her will rebelled. She did not want to shake the hand of this man who had caused her and all the other prisoners so much suffering. She wanted to walk away and repudiate his efforts.

But she could not. She could not on the one hand preach a message of forgiveness, and then refuse to offer that forgiveness to others, no matter how hurt she had felt by them!

Her hand still refused to move. She breathed a prayer for help, and thrust out her hand to meet the hand of the man. She realised that action often precedes feelings. If she could at least put her hand out, she was then going to rely on God to supply the feeling of forgiveness she couldn't personally muster.

Corrie was completely amazed by the feeling that filled her. From the moment her hand reached out towards the man's hand, a feeling of warmth radiated from her shoulder down her arm.

The words tumbled out of her mouth, and she realised that she meant them: 'I forgive you, brother!'

She knew that this demonstration of love and forgiveness had not come from her. She had tried of her own will, and failed. This love had come from God. He had enabled her to experience the feeling of forgiveness that she did not have the will to do herself. Her part had been to put out her hand.

She had made the 'horse' ready for battle, but the victory belonged to the Lord!

So it is with us. Sometimes our feelings don't line up with the Spirit fruit way. Sometimes all we can achieve is a prayer for help, and a tentative step of action. We have to leave it with God to supply the rest, when and how He sees fit.

The fruit He wants to see in us is a desire to conform our will to His way. Success and triumph over our weaknesses will be His victory, not ours. Maybe the victory over our feelings, or disinclination, won't be as instantaneous as it seems it was for

Corrie. Maybe our negative feelings and sin struggle are going to take a much longer time for an overhaul.

One lady I know has told me of her struggle with alcoholism. When she gave her life to Christ, her struggle did not instantly end. She described it as: 'A bottle of drink in one hand, and a Bible in the other. Eventually the Bible won!' For her, the struggle over her weakness and temptation took time and a consistent effort to stay focused on God's Word.

She made her 'horse' ready for battle against her alcohol problem, and when the time was right, God gave her the victory.

This chapter began with a contemplation of the fruit of the Spirit. Love is the ultimate Spirit fruit that we want to have growing in our lives, and transforming our actions. "Love never fails", 1 Corinthians 13 tells us. Love is the most excellent way. Faith, Hope and Love remain, and the greatest of these is Love.

I invite you to join me in prayerful meditation on the sentiments of love from 1 Corinthians 13 at the conclusion of this chapter. May God's Most Excellent Way – the way of love – grow in us and shine out of us, to His honour, and His glory. May love permeate our lives, filling us with the warmth and the glow of God's great love for us. May it overflow from a heart that is grateful for the love we have ourselves received. May that love be extended to those around us.

God delights in our desire to want to walk in step with His Spirit. He has given us everything we need to help us in this process. He has shown us the rotten flesh fruit that needs to be got rid of. He has told us what 'good clothes' to wear. He has provided us with armour to help protect our growth. He has told us what sort of things to think about to have healthy minds. He has provided us with the delightful Spirit fruit of joy to give us courage and a healthy inner glow. He partners with us through His Spirit to help us in our weakness. He gives us the ability to achieve what we cannot do alone. He has shown us love, and what love looks like. And most precious of all, He has provided us with our Lord Jesus, to walk alongside us, cheer us along, empathise with our weaknesses, show us the way, and to love us – warts and all.

Praise be to God for His extravagant gift of love!

"But the fruit of the Spirit is love, joy, peace, forbearance, kindness, goodness, faithfulness, gentleness and self-control. Against such things there is no law. Those who belong to Christ Jesus have crucified the flesh with its passions and desires. Since we live by the Spirit, let us keep in step with the Spirit" (Galatians 5:22-25).

The transforming journey is a process of time,
Needing courage to start the spiritual climb.
He's supplied all the means, and provided the way,
To live life in tune, to be keen to obey.

So I want to give Thanks for all God has done,
He's shown me my value, in the gift of His Son.
He's helping me grow, and He's changing my heart,
I see beauty in what He has planned from the start!

In a nutshell:

- Walking in step with the Spirit requires us to become empty to the way of the flesh.

- The fruit of the Spirit in our lives is an outward marker of inward change.

- God's Word supplies us with disciplines and instruction as to how we can protect and grow good Spirit fruit.

- These include discipline in our thoughts, the right 'clothes' to wear, protective armour, growth and joy.

- Recognising and receiving God's love in our lives helps us give that love out to others also.

Prayer time:

'Dear Lord, please shine the light of your Spirit on my life, and awaken love in me as you have designed it to be. Please work on my moments of impatience, and where I am lacking in kindness. Please remove envy, boasting, pride and rudeness from my life, so that love can live triumphantly. Please work on my self-centredness, moments of anger, or the times where I delight in evil, and rehearse the wrongs of others. All of these I lay before you as love-inhibitors.

Instead, may I rejoice in truth. May I desire to protect. May trust, hope and perseverance triumph over all those things that would pull me down and stifle love. May love never fail!

Amen'

"Love is patient, love is kind. It does not envy, it does not boast, it is not proud. It does not dishonour others, it is not self-seeking, it is not easily angered, it keeps no record of wrongs. Love does not delight in evil but rejoices with the truth. It always protects, always trusts, always hopes, always perseveres. Love never fails" (1 Corinthians 13:4-8).

Chapter 21

Section Two conclusion

A S we began Section Two, the caterpillars were at the point of significant change. They had eaten their way to become large caterpillars, ready for the next step of their transformation.

They would now no longer be identified as caterpillars. They would hang in a vulnerable in-between liquid state, in the form of a chrysalis. The liquid would contain a few key elements of the original caterpillar; which would become the basis of the eventual butterfly. This stage of change would take a number of days to complete, during which time some momentous changes would take place inside the chrysalis. By the time we reached our last chapter, the chrysalis was empty. It had served its purpose and the creature inside had emerged. We are yet to see what the newly emerged creature looks like. We will soon. But first let's recap on what our own choices of change might look like.

This part of our change journey is best summarised as 'increasing by decreasing'. The decision we have been faced with is the choice of letting go of self, or clinging on to self. Letting go of self means that we are prepared to diminish in the ways of the flesh. It also means that we will be in a better position to increase in the ways of the Spirit.

Letting go of self is a significant milestone for our transformation. It's where we can let go of our own 'identity' so that we can take on Christ's identity.

Incredible as it sounds, the more we diminish in the ways of our natural flesh, the more we will increase in value. "Those who humble themselves will be exalted."

The alternative is to stay clinging to our own identity, conformed to the world's pattern of Me, Myself and I. This is the way of our natural flesh. It is the way we exalt ourselves; but it leaves no room for God to exalt us. This would be like a caterpillar remaining as a caterpillar; a large flight-less grub!

Let us remind ourselves that God loves us as we are. But He loves us too much to leave us that way!

He wants us to move on to this next phase of change, and He has provided us with help and encouragement for every step of the journey. We see this particularly through our Lord Jesus Christ. He was sent to show us the way, experience our weaknesses, bear our sins, defeat sin, open the door for forgiveness, love us immensely, and show us what grace looks like. He is now seated at his Father's right hand, cheering us on, empathising with our faltering steps, and encouraging us to keep going.

What a beautiful gift!

Our journey of decreasing in the way of self has meant that we have had to open the door of our heart. This is a very vulnerable thing to do. Some of us have had our hearts closed and barred for years. Perhaps there are particularly painful and ugly things inside that we prefer not to face. But opening the door of our heart is a necessary part of the process of change and healing. Facing our weaknesses, acknowledging them, submitting to the healing work of the Master Physician, seeking forgiveness and receiving grace, are all pivotal for our transformation.

Maybe there has been some painful cutting, pruning, and shaping that has had to happen. Perhaps there has been some muck that has needed digging or scraping out.

In much the same way as a surgeon has to remove the diseased or unhealthy parts in the body during surgery, so we also need to have the unhealthy parts of us cleansed so that we are open to healing in our mind and heart. There might be some pain; but it's for an overall greater gain.

Finally, we have considered how Faith, Hope and Love play a major part in the transformation process.

Faith is necessary for our spiritual journey.

> "And without faith it is impossible to please God, because anyone who comes to him must believe that he exists and that he rewards those who earnestly seek him" (Hebrews 11:6).

Faith is built on a belief that God has a particular direction for us. Faith requires us to act on that belief. Faith in action, helps us to let go of those things in our heart that go against the way of the Spirit.

We need hope to hold on to during those hard, hot, painful or uncomfortable moments of trial as God grows our faith.

There will be a better day ahead, but we must keep holding on to hope and trust God to see us through the difficult times.

> "Not only so, but we also glory in our sufferings, because we know that suffering produces perseverance; perseverance character; and character, hope. And hope does not put us to shame, because God's love has been poured out into our hearts ..." (Romans 5:3-5).

Love. This beautiful attribute leads the way in Spirit fruit. It's like an outer layer that encompasses all the other attributes of the fruit of the Spirit. It wraps them all up in a beautiful package. We need love in our lives – to receive it, and to show it!

"Dear friends, let us love one another, for love comes from God. Everyone who loves has been born of God and knows God. Whoever does not love does not know God, because God is love. This is how God showed his love among us: He sent his one and only Son into the world that we might live through him" (1 John 4:7-9).

Let us finish this short recap with a few rousing and inspiring verses from the book of Hebrews:

"Therefore, brothers and sisters, since we have confidence to enter the Most Holy Place by the blood of Jesus, by a new and living way opened for us through the curtain, that is, his body, and since we have a great priest over the house of God, let us draw near to God with a sincere heart with the full assurance that faith brings, having our hearts sprinkled to cleanse us from a guilty conscience and having our bodies washed with pure water. Let us hold unswervingly to the hope we profess, for he who promised is faithful" (Hebrews 10:19-23).

Now it's time to take a look at what has emerged from its chrysalis. Let's see, and marvel, at what change has occurred.

Chapter 22

Revealing the butterfly

"He has made everything beautiful in its time" (Ecclesiastes 3:11).

"And we, who with unveiled faces contemplate the Lord's glory, are being transformed into his image with ever-increasing glory, which comes from the Lord, who is the Spirit" (2 Corinthians 3:18)

ON the leaf of its swan plant, not far from its empty chrysalis, stood the newly emerged butterfly. It was brand new and beautiful in form, vibrant in colour.

Its wings were uniform, healthy and strong. Even now, as we watch, it stretches its wings gracefully to make them ready for flight. This beautiful little creature will shortly be able to leave its leaf for a new life; an air-bound life.

No longer confined to its narrow little world of swan plant, it will have new horizons to explore. It is now well on the road towards fulfilling its role; to be all that it was designed to be.

It has successfully come through its metamorphosis to become the lovely little creature we can now see. Its new life has begun.

As we linger watchfully with this newly emerged butterfly, we can marvel at the process that has brought it to this point. We can experience a sense of celebration for it, that all the challenges that the small caterpillar may have encountered throughout its various changes have been successfully navigated.

This is truly a great wonder of transformation. How satisfying it is.

Do you remember, from our first chapter, the other butterfly that had emerged? Sadly, that butterfly had deformed wings, which made it incapable of being all that it could be. It had gone through a process of change that, for whatever reason, hadn't quite achieved a full and complete transformation.

The picture of transformation that we have seen from the two butterflies has shown us what successful change looked like in one butterfly, but how disappointing the outcome was in the other.

A butterfly has little choice as to how its transformation turns out. There are many unavoidable factors that play into the final picture.

It is not the same for us. We have choices. Every choice we make affects what we become. We can choose the way of the world, that will help us become more flesh-centred, or we can choose the way of God, which helps us become more Christ-centred.

As life goes on, we will all change. It is inevitable.

One or other of the options will eventually become the more dominant one. The question we need to ask ourselves is: Which transformation outcome do I want?

Oh that we may all choose the first option:

"And we, who with unveiled faces contemplate the Lord's glory, are being transformed into his image with ever-increasing glory, which comes from the Lord, who is the Spirit" (2 Corinthians 3:18).

To be transformed into His "image", His likeness, we must want to look less like the world's likeness!

A strong thread of value has emerged from our thoughts on transformation. Our value has been established through God's abundant love. He wants us. He loves us. We have seen how gratitude, and care of our natural bodies enhances value in our lives. Purposeful living has given us a chance to grow value in our lives. Our value now has opportunity to increase through us decreasing to self.

As we look at our lives may we be able to see the beauty and love that God has lavished on us, that tells us that we are wanted, loved and have purpose. It is this that helps us accept that, although we are not perfect, we can be forgiven and made righteous.

Accepting and seeing our value from God helps us gain a new perspective.

These have been life-changing concepts for me personally. As I am learning to see how much God loves me, and wants me to succeed, I am finding a greater strength to relinquish those false foundations of value that I had previously relied on. It is an ongoing journey of change, with steps that sometimes falter more than I would like; but I am grateful that God continues to be patient with me throughout it!

So here we are. In many ways, transformation for us will not be a completed work until Christ returns. In the meanwhile, we are a work in progress. Let us take a look back over our lives and see where our choices are taking us. Are our choices making us stay conformed to the world, which is passing away, and subject to sin and death? Or are our choices saying 'yes' to God's work in our lives; to the renewing of our minds, and 'yes' to the Spirit pathway?

One path leads to healthy change; or healthy 'wings' as it were. The other path leads to unfulfilled potential; an inability to be all that we could be.

As we reveal the butterfly of our lives, let us think carefully about what we want that to look like. By the Lord's help and grace we can become all that we were designed to be.

One day this butterfly will fly. Transformation will be complete. What we are now is nothing like what we will be. What we will eventually be, in our fully transformed state, is beyond comprehension.

Here are a few verses to keep reminding ourselves of what that will look like one day:

"The body that is sown is perishable, it is raised imperishable; it is sown in dishonour, it is raised in glory; it is sown in weakness, it is raised in power; it is sown a natural body, it is raised a spiritual body ... We will not all sleep, but we will all be changed – in a flash, in the twinkling of an eye, at the last trumpet ... Just as we have borne the likeness of the earthly man, so shall we bear the likeness of the heavenly man" (1 Corinthians 15:42-44,49,51,52).

"But our citizenship is in heaven. And we eagerly await a Saviour from there, the Lord Jesus Christ, who by the power that enables him to bring everything under his control, will transform our lowly bodies so that they will be like his glorious body" (Philippians 3:20,21).

"Dear friends, now we are children of God, and what we will be has not yet been made known. But we know that when Christ appears, we shall be like him, for we shall see him as he is. All who have this hope in him purify themselves, just as he is pure" (1 John 3:2,3).

At that time, we who are currently imperfect, will be made perfect. We will be as different as a seed is from the flower it later becomes. We will be as different as a caterpillar is from a butterfly. On that day, we will be complete. It will be beyond amazing!

Meanwhile, dear fellow traveller on a journey of transformation, there is work to be done. May we stand together, as we support each other to change and grow, in preparation for that final transformation.

"Therefore, my dear [sisters], stand firm. Let nothing move you. Always give yourselves fully to the work of the Lord, because you know that your labour in the Lord is not in vain" (1 Corinthians 15:58).

God bless you on your transformation journey.

"We shall be like him." O how rich the promise;
    What greater could our Father's love prepare?
Few are the words, and softly are they spoken,
    But who shall tell the blessings hidden there?

"We shall be like him" – pure in heart, and sinless;
    But his redeeming mercy ends not there;
These bodies like to his shall then be fashioned,
    And we his resurrection glory share. (Hymn 388)

Chapter 23

Poem – 'Revealing the Butterfly'

I looked in the mirror, and fell to despair,
What pouchy tired eyes, and distinctly grey hair!
Nose kind of large, and wrinkles defined,
That was only the beginning, what more could I find?

I head to the shops, maybe I'll feel better there,
Perhaps retail therapy can rid my despair.
But time at the shops seems to only make worse
The me-esteem problem that's such a curse!

Now, the lady in front, she helps me feel better,
Compared to her, I'm quite a go-getter!
That fills me with hope – and it's more than a glimmer,
For standing by her, I'm certainly slimmer!

But confidence tumbles as I look to my right,
The manicured beauty whose demeanour is bright.
Compared to her, I'm awkward and plain,
Can't I be more like her? is a common refrain.

'Dear Lord', I declare, 'I'm in a bit of a bind.
Can you show me the way, please help me to find,
The right way to see myself, a healthy way to be …
For I'm struggling, Lord, in accepting me!'

And the Father looked down from His throne on high,
He said, 'Come to me child, come and draw nigh,
I will show you your worth – way beyond compare,
Child, don't look to others, don't fall to despair!'

He showed me a garden, perfect and new,
A man and woman within, the only two.
'Look closely', He said, 'If only you could tell,
You too, like them, I've made "wonderfully well"!'

I realised how ungrateful to Him I must seem,
A thankful heart I must grow, if I want to redeem
Lost time and perspective – a new way to see,
With God's view as my focus – a right way to be.

'Be thankful in all things', is what He has said.
It now depends on what my thoughts are fed.
For sure, it's not easy, but victory is near,
With joy a reward for a heart full of cheer!

'Trust me in this', He said, 'for I have a great plan,
A life of purpose for you, as for all of man.
Place your confidence now, in what I can do,
For you, and with you, it surely is true!'

I paused to reflect on what I was learning –
Confidence in God's purpose is what I'm discerning.
Accepting how He has made me to be,
Without need to compare, for He's uniquely made me!

'But don't be complacent', I now hear Him say,
'There's something within you that's not so okay!
Your form, it is true, is made wonderfully well,
But that heart that you've got needs some change, I can
tell!'

'Do you mean a heart transplant?' I hear my voice squeak,
'That's major business, I'm afraid I'm too weak!
Will it hurt, are you gentle? There's so much to ask ...
I'm sorry to doubt, but can I trust you this task?'

'Be assured', the Lord said, 'my ways you can trust,
Look to Jesus, follow him, be like him, it's a must!
Come to know him, and see just how great is my love,
For through him I offer you grace from above!'

The heart of the matter, I see, is to trust,
A life of faith in God is also a must!
'Lord, courage I need, to allow this to be,
For faith must be active, please help me to see.'

'There's another thing child', I hear the Lord say,
'Times will come in your life when I strip things away,
A furnace of fire it may feel it can be,
It's called refining, you see, to help draw you to me.'

'Take a teacup, for instance, to help you compare,
Its beauty is made with design and great care,
But once it was just a great lump of dry clay,
Until it was moulded and shaped in this way.'

'You too, like this cup, need some shaping to grow,
It may feel like it hurts, but I want you to know,
I really do know just what I am doing,
It's going to take time, but your heart is renewing!'

The transforming journey is a process of time,
Needing courage to start the spiritual climb.
He's supplied all the means, and provided the way,
To live life in tune, to be keen to obey.

I want to give thanks for all God has done,
He's shown me my value in the gift of His Son.
He's helping me grow, and He's changing my heart,
I see beauty in what He has planned from the start!

When a butterfly emerges, with wings that are strong,
We see success in the process, with nothing gone wrong.
When Jesus returns, may he find this to be –
Us, like a butterfly, changed and now free!

Sharon Prins

Scripture index